All things man-made shall pass away;
This verse will fade, as I one day . . . but

Mountains
Are
Forever

by Leroy Sossamon

This book is dedicated
to all those who love these mountains.

Books by Leroy Sossamon:
FALLING SKY
BACKSIDE OF HEAVEN
THESE MY MOUNTAINS, THIS MY LAND
MOUNTAINS ARE FOREVER

Acknowledgment:

A special thank you to Dora Mangum,
Don and May Stewart for their help.

Some poems previously published in
MOUNTAIN LIFE & WORK, Berea, Ky.
THE SMOKY MOUNTAIN TIMES
FALLING SKY
BACKSIDE OF HEAVEN
MODERN AMERICAN POETRY, 1935
IMPORTANT AMERICAN POETS, 1935

First printing, July, 2001

THE VILLAGE PRESS
Bryson City, North Carolina, 28713

Composition by Rainbow Graphics

Manufactured in the USA by
Quebecor World Books.

MOUNTAINS ARE FOREVER

Once long ago a masterpiece
I built out on the beach;
I thought I placed it carefully
Just back of water's reach.
But while I was away one day
A Wind came swishing by
And joined the Waves—

                      They rushed ashore,
Forced high tide way too high.
My loving labor sifted down
To one great heap of sand,
And when that high tide sloshed away
These few shells marked my land.

I planted shrubs, flowers galore
To pretty up my lawn;
Then came a storm;

                   When I awoke
My pretties all were gone.
I watched the clouds paint lovely hues,
Splash colors on blue sky,
But just before I wrote my notes
Their beauty slipped me by.

I shaped a poem in my sleep,
And judged it super fine,
But next morning when I awoke
I recalled not one line.
I thought a deed my neighbor did
Deserved a huge *thank you,*
But the day I did not thank him,
He died! What could I do?

Cotton candy melts fast away
With one small child's soft touch;
Our happy times soon fade away
In memory

And much
As we might plan always to keep
Some moment *status quo*
Age tends to smudge the picture and
Down road we will not know.

Our patched routine of daily life
Will change from day to day;
Our plans sink deep in memory
And hide out, lost away.
Our dearest friends, the faces all
That fill our hearts with joy
Go, one by one, and disappear
As some child's long-lost toy.

Thus to forget is part of life,
And thereby we are blessed;
It means our most unhappy times
Are also laid to rest.
We then can face a new daybreak
Without our old sorrow;
Memory's garden, flush with dew,
Brings us new tomorrow.
And when depressed we gain new peace
By looking to the hills,
While just above, in smoky haze,
Mountains do soldier drills.

They stand today as yesterday,
Ten thousand years the same,
Tall sentinels marking Time's highway,
And man's low flick'ring fame.

These hills are like young girls in spring
With flowers in their hair,
Decked out for summer, dressed in green;
Happy and tall; they care!
Come fall they wear their colors bright

To chase dark wint'ry hues;
They cheer us up with cozy days
And take away our blues.

So with His mountains God shows us
In terms we understand
Where we can spend Eternity;
The address: Promise Land.

To bolster faith we look and see
God's mountains still out there,
Dressed out in Life's serene make-up
With eagles in their hair.

Hand-maidens to our Mountains tall
These hills fail us never;
For we now know, and God will show,
Mountains are forever!

Man-made shall pass, we've long been told;
Nothing could be truer,
But when man-made has passed to dust,
God's mountains will endure!

I'M ON MY WAY

Leave one small star on twinkle, Lord,
Out by your big back door,
'Cause I'm as usual runnin' late,
My corns are awful sore.
I'll just slip in, skip the Goodnight,
Prayers already said;
I'm so worn out findin' my way,
I'll just go in to bed.

Back down on earth I lost a shoe
Runnin' from Ol' Devil;

That sucker nearly caught me too;
His playin' field's un-level!
I'm comin' home. I need a rest.
Po' ol' raggety me!
So prop that back door open wide
'Cause I don't have a key!

Life down on Earth was gettin' worse,
At times I thought to quit.
You need to set them straight down there——
Soft money's partly it!
Why, once on Earth I had to hide
For weeks and weeks,
                    You see
I only wanted some firewood,
But cut their Hangin' Tree.
Had to put off my funeral too;
This Near-Blind mistook me.
The D.A. said "He's guilty, Sir!"
That Jedge agreed.
                    Oh, me!
Watch out fer me. Keep open door;
Make some hot-tea toddy;
I'll rest the night, then shoot some stars;
Love yuh! Everbody!

EMIT'S CURSE

Hell-smell, brimstone, sheer terror, mad curses!
Time doesn't end,
                It slowly reverses!
In one great gorging of feathers and pelf
Foolish and blinded, Emit's choking himself.
Lacking common sense, he tries to spoof,
Drunk on raw power, he shows no proof,

Then with great gulps of poison and slime
Emit goes for broke—

                    He butchers Time!
So, it's technology and not the snake,
Nor this time the apple, for heaven's sake.
It's bin Laden, Iraq, and Iran too,
Adding new vintage to old Devil brew;
It's Saddam Hussein and his mad men who
Trick Palestine, Israel,
                    The Arab,
                              The Jew.

It's diplomats, sorcery, ships bombed at sea,
A hovering cloud of terror to be.
It's little Afghanistan walking tall,
Hiding mad men who answer Terror's call;
It's Clinton's smoothing over where Hell's cauldrons boil;
It's water, global warming, the world fight for oil.
Hell boils over with a broken thermostat;
And we march on to slaughter, rat-a-tat-tat!

We're all guilty.
                    We've set out world ablaze
With new super-tech and new strange ways.
Emit's climbers reach up, groping the stars;
Space-Age travelers kick down Heavens bars.
Emit keeps reversing. We teeter on the edge!
We must get armed; we must tighten the wedge!
Then Emit pulls the plug!

                    He reinvents Sin,
And we can't dent his armor with our sleeves turned in!
The doors of old Hell are propped open wide.
We cry from the mountain
                    Where can we hide?
It's a bold hi-jacking!

Democracy
Is shoved to the pit.
                    A final act, We
Can give these lost Souls last turf to tread on
As they march lock-step to
                              Armageddon!
Help!
      Stop mad Emit who seeks to take us,
Destroy our Planet, shape and remake us.
We're roaring off the edge!
                              That's Hell we see.
Not title for a book, not history.
Disheveled, disoriented, frozen in Emit's track,
We're breaking through Hell, and no coming back!
Democracy was best and we're letting it sour.
No one gets to Heaven who A-bombs the tower!

We can't slay this beast.

            When all's said and done
We only yell the warning,

            Then we run!
And when the mountains no longer hide us,
Doomsday will come and lie down beside us.

Part I

THE AMERICANS   THE MAKING OF A NATION

God knows how, but they were to walk invincible;
        shadowed in the strength of a few strapping, homespun,
        rifle-toting prophets; flanked by their many-petticoated
        do-gooders who kept them on the prod.

They were to build whole new towns nor ask a jail;
cross rivers, top mountains, nor know to fail,
as they spread over this vast tumbleweed sod.
Indians had to be fought, yesterday's dead buried,
penance paid to a stern, just God.

Till out of their iron will molded rock hard, wind-tempered,
sun-mellowed and pliant from use,
they fell heir to the soles of our heritage;
they fashioned our ten-league boots.

These boots were laced in shimmering rail chasing away to
the Pacific rainbow; they outran the panting pony
express, took over the United States mail, scattered the
red man with wild, shrill whistle toots.

They were made to go chugging off with cattle, motors and
derby-hat drummers; hauling calico, woolens, sixguns,
western cowboy hats and loud-striped, peg-legged suits.

Later, others were to stand wide-footed between sweat-stained
plow handles and look up in awe at the frail wings of
Lindbergh, Corrigan, Post and Rogers,
Amelia Earhart and all the rest.

They lived through two great wars; no longer heard above
the roar of tractors and whirring combines the great
jet-screaming eagles out of Wichita, Kansas City and
Chicago, bound for Hawaii, Tokyo and points west.

This had become the milk run. Now they were busy watching
television, hearing about Canaveral, seeing gleaming
slender rocket-propelled space ships, reading orbit
schedules, talking Venus shots, wondering when we
would put an astronaut in space and who would be first
to the moon.
The future would be their best.

Part II

AMERICA,   A NATION'S REBIRTH

From the vast expanse of Texas to Frost's
    New Hampshire hills;
From the mighty Mississippi to the East's huge steel mills;
West to the world's bread basket; Detroit with her
    magic wheels;
Chicago, butcher to the world; New York, maker of deals.
Hollywood, weaver of tall dreams that dwarf reality;
But now we turn their magic cloth to clothes for you and me!

Fat Lady sings her fateful song; we rush to change the stage;
The stars and stripes unfurl above and signal our new age!
The job has grown to Texan-size, but Texas heard our call;
A bright new nation moves to term.

                                        Democracy walks tall!

No longer will we build a fence and safely hide behind it;
Our Freedom walks before us, that all a world may find it.

The Space Age and the Internet join Man to help him find
And cut away old time-aged chains that weigh down
    Man's keen mind.
In strength but with humility we make our Nation strong.
With moving finger Time rewrites; the poet sings along.
History strides across our stage to open wide new gates!
God Bless America!
                        President Bush!
                                These United States!

ROBERT FROST AND HIS SNOWY WOOD

It was early on in morning I came back to this wood.
Oh, such a day for making tracks or wondering where one should.
The storm-fed snow of yesterday lay peaceful now and still,
Seeming to say, *come, come and play, make tracks up, down my hill.*

Yes, Mr. Frost you should have stayed, matched tracks with me
    that day;
Instead some strange mood hexed you and you hurried on
    your way.
If you had stayed we could have played in fresh new crunchy
    snow;
And all that time you could tell me the things I need to know:
How the muse can lift you up, plant diamonds in fresh dew,
Or slow the mind and drag you down when no phrase quite
    will do.
Please tell me, Sir, did poetry flow from your mind full clad?
Or sometimes did you dig and search and thought you would
    go mad?

As I stood there this strange feeling slipped up and took my mind;
New snow swirled all about me; its brightness struck me blind.
I felt only cold wet snow—
                                'Til slowly came to view
A figure walking toward me—
                                Oh, Mr. Frost, 'twas you!
I heard your voice:
                    On yesterday I gladly would have stayed,
But all those vows, the promises I knew that I had made
Came back to haunt my tortured mind—
                                Though much I needed sleep,
The vow, the promise long since made I thought I had to keep.

Then, Mr. Frost, you waved Goodbye, slow-fading through
    thick snow.
I felt sad, but somewhat glad, you chose me first to know.
Now I can re-read your work, mind at ease knowing
That when we meet again in snow, white and thick and
    blowing,
You'll tell me all about the farm, and how it nurtured you—
And If I found myself a farm, would it inspire me too?

Why, Mr. Frost! You still are there! You turned! You waved
    your cap!
The déjà vu! This meeting you! We both must take our nap!

POET, BUILD ME A SONG

I want a Poet
To make me a song.
  Not in jasmine ink
  On paper pale pink
In facile meter or long;
But build the song!

Fashion it life-like;
Breathe in it part
Of the sinewy strength
In a nation's great heart.

And, Poet, think not
For even one minute
That curses and sweat
Cannot be in it.

Build to the plan
Though Critics gore us,
For, Poet, the people
Must sing this chorus!
Build in it strife,
Battles lost, won;
Breathe in it life,
And tasks nobly done.

Build the song
A people may feel,
May see in its rhythm
The forging of steel,
May hear in its singing
The song of the mill,
May out of its music
Glean courage, new will,

That topping the Mountain
To beauty below

The people may sing it,
And singing it, know
That out of its fullness
As they trudge along
Flow fountains of courage.
Poet, the song!

HOW CAME THE HILLS

On the sixth day
God sorted His clay
And thought it had spoiled;
He threw it away.
But a mountainside
With valleys green
And snow-capped peaks
All in between,
And a flowery glade
With green-grassed sod
Sprang up and blossomed.
"Selah!" said God
On the seventh day,
"That beauty-forsaken
Hard lump of clay
Made the noblest work
Of all my week;
My throne shall be
This mountain peak!"

CONFUSED

Life can be a lightning bolt,
Often without the thunder.
Quick flash!
          Deep shock!
                    Sudden jolt!
It makes one think,
          And wonder:

Is this the start?

The end?

The night?

Are we top-side?   Or under?

TRACKS

A track is a simple thing.

I know.

I've made millions in fresh snow.
How clear they were those tracks each day!
But when again I chanced that way
The tracks were gone!

Some will say

They never were,

That history

Will make no note of them or me,
But, Wilful Child, I still must go
Along those same paths, tracking snow.

One day we met at this strange place.
I thought we did!

You wore no face.

But tracks we made that day will blend
With yet more tracks at river's end.

Tracks all must fade, we understand;
Buried in Time, covered by sand,
Lifted with water's steady flow,
Or some high tide.

We'll never know

Whose track we trampled,

In what snow.

And if unseen, who is to know?

One will know.

Our Friend, our Backer,

The Man upstairs,

The Master Tracker.

THE TWO ROADS

I came to the place.
                Two roads met;
It seemed I have been there before.
No sign stood to guide me, and yet
My instinct was telling me more.

Which road to go? The high? The low?
Should I try for the hills above,
Or drop to the valley out of the snow
For an easy choice I would love?

I thought: Frost, which way did you go?
Are you out there climbing still?
No! You would never walk so slow;
For yours was a stubborn will.

But maybe you met low snow clouds,
Strong winds, no way to go;
You fell in a drift. Even worse,
Stiff frozen in deep snow.

I decided: Hurry back through time,
To that rock-strewn farm and owner;
Dig him from the snow; say *Man, let's go!*
He'd say, Oh! No! I'm a loner!

TIME, PAST OR FUTURE, IS FOREVER *NOW*

I chose the road less traveled by
    And hurried on my way
To find some magic overlook
    And call back yesterday.
I should have known nothing could change
    Footsteps made in the Past;
Life's two great wheels had caught me up
    Then locked me down too fast.

13

I s'pose some way I hoped to find
    A path 'til now unseen;
And Time could cut a bit of slack
    Where *Now* lies wedged between.
Then all at once somewhere down road
    I stopped short, turned about;
Frost too had once walked down this road,
    But let no secret out.

And I stood now on that same spot,
    Gazed down along life's road;
Realized that heart could not restart
    Or change what Time bestowed.
Wheels past, wheels Future, could not move
    If wedged between is *Now*
With no eraser for Time's pen
    Or no hint as to how.

Trapped!
        No! I thought, I'll look ahead.
    The Future leave to me!
But Frost said *No! Past cannot change,*
    And Future's yet to be!
Time's two great wheels still hold you fast—
    And that's Finality!
The wheels squeak, but never speak—
    And that's Eternity!

A Celebration of The Great Smoky Mountains
and the Mountain Poet who has lived among them,
loved them for more than three score years and
ten. His fourth book, MOUNTAINS ARE FOREVER,
for whatever its worth, Is a brave tribute to both the
mountains and the man.

Climbing the mountain nearing home

The focus of man's mortality comes more clearly into view,
And my list grows longer more rapidly of undone things to do

NIGHT COMES TO THE BLUE RIDGE

Evening beds down the Blue Ridge
   In soft blankets of cloud.
I gaze there in wond'rous awe
   And thank God, head unbowed,
That mountains, clouds, trees and all,
   Though His in wisdom planned,
Are ours to use.
            We still call
These our Mountains, This our Land.

COMPENSATED

Now Hope nests high on the mountain's wild side,
   Now flutters in vales of despair;
But without the valleys how should Hope know
   That the beautiful hills were there?

MOUNTAIN BANDIT

Day has gathered twilight to dusk
   In frenzied, climbing toil,
And the reaching hands of the midnight musk
   Reek with lantern oil.

Yet out from the still night swells a chord
   Whose music will not be done—
A song of peace, the battle's reward
   That the day has never won.

The shadows open, letting
   Forth a young moon's light;
And sleep, old in forgetting,
   Pillows lonely night.

LOST LOVE

Last night's young moon touched tenderly
   These lonely smoky peaks;
Last night's cool breezes brought to me
   The memory of weeks
And months and years that now are gone;
   Fond hopes, forgotten fears;
Memory of some long last look,
   The heartache of young tears.

Then last night's same moon climbed afar
   To dwarf the highest peak,
Leaving but dark silhouettes—
   No face, no lips to speak;

Just many mountains all alike
　　Through distant smoky haze,
As when some tourist stops his car
　　But in a moment's gaze
Finds scarcely passing interest,
　　So through the night drives on
Till moon is spent, till hills awake
　　To find another dawn.

SKYLADY

Proudly and
So high she stands
Like some great romping girl,
Gathering up
Her tree-lined skirts
Above the village swirl.

Wistfully
She looks down
Upon our village life,
But daughter of
The stars is she,
And to the moon a wife.

In summer's low
And lovely dress,
With dew drops in her hair,
A mystic rhythm
Poet-bred
My hungering soul reads there.

Now I see
Her distantly
Against the black night sky;
The earth beneath
Her cretonned stool,
Earth's dwellers ants, as I.

And like some moth
On window's ledge
I long to court her favor;
To climb into
Her lap and kiss
And thank the stars who gave her.

In winter still
I gaze at her
And then at last I know—
Perfect rhythm
Does with rhyme
What mountains do with snow.

MOUNTAIN FALL

Gay foliage fills these thousand hills
   With richest red and brown;
Bright golds and yellows fit for kings
   Are over all the town.

No winding way but now will lead
   To new majestic views,
Where yet more mountains lie fresh dipped
   In long-lost rainbow hues.

For truly God our Smokies gave
   First choice in richest color,
Leaving all who later chose
   A choice much the duller.

I will lift up mine eyes unto the hills
from whence cometh my help.
               Psalms 121

MOUNTAINS

I live in a valley.
Mountains above
Watch over me.

And how I love
To know these mountains are such part
And parcel of me.
How my heart
Is lifted when in hour of need,
Though sorely tried by man's small greed
God's strength flows through these wooded hills
And peace once more my tired heart fills.

Or if in spirit free I fly,
These mountain summits, tall as sky,
Spread all around and under me
Until as far as eye can see,
Or Soul can touch, or heaven fill,
Their greener pastures feed me still.

These mountains comfort me.
My head
Shall seek them for its nightly bed.
Though Soul may thirst, clear mountain flow
Brings sweet waters.
Though I should go
Alone, apart from foe or friend,
Mountains still call to me.
The end
May well be here.
My valley's floor
Could be for me Life's final door.
But, victor yet o've fates to be,
My faithful hills will shelter me!

I THRILL TO SEE A MOUNTAIN

I thrill to see a mountain decked with buds: like some young
    lover
  Who listens with throbbing heart for her mate's quick
    step in spring;

And, loving without measure, spreads for his approach a cover
    Of grasses and flowers; the music of a glad brook's
        whispering;
Whose untamed spirit finds first its peace beneath his strong
        caress;
    Whose yearning soul's fulfilment is the bearing of his seed;
Who, last a buxom matron in her flowing leafy dress,
    Finds a fuller sweetness in her offspring's every need.

I thrill to see a mountain: Gaunt, matured, crested with snow;
    Hips full from the weight of forest-bearing;
Wrinkled and furrowed with the tears of the gods, that go
    To join on some far plain the river; sharing
With unstinted motherliness the substance of her being
    To raise her progeny for the big pulp mills;
And then scarce yet their shade a comfort, seeing
    Through her mother grief only her barren hills.

I thrill to see a mountain: Come to winter's bareness
    Clad somberly in mourning for her dead and fallen leaves;
Yet magnificent in her faith, and bearing an awareness
    Of triumph immortal; for her mountain soul believes
Her trees still live in service; that whispering rills, so soon spent,
    Only changed their form and went away to turn the
        roaring mills;
That even she will sometime sprout a valley's grain; so, content,
    She waits it out in peace among her faithful hills.

MOUNTAINS AT EVENING

These are my mountains, this is my land . . . .
Oh, excuse me, God.
                Please understand . . . .
I created no mountains tall;
I really don't own them at all.

It's just that I get carried away
When near the close of a blue-sky day
I stand atop this mountain peak,

Watch sunset fade and wild birds seek
Their night cover of laurel trees;
Feel the cool of a playful breeze;
See the lights wink on back in the town
Where dusk lies soft as blankets of down—
When my path leads home down through the pine,
Somehow I feel these mountains are mine.

WINTER BIRCH

Birch are meant for snow-white hills
and crystalled streams in winter.
birch were sent to seek blue sky;
to hold over earth their jewelled parasol
of March nights and glittering, moon-lit frost.

Birch are purely wasted in summer.
Silvery tall,
their white-stemmed shade
is but a whisper
blowing hot in August's breath.

Then I long to see snow covering
my peaceful hills once more,
with the birch—
the tall white birch—
gracing great packages of God's rich earth,
tied with patched blue sky.

Love the stalwart, shady oak?
Yes, Lord, I try.
But it's the birch that catch my eye.

THOSE FAR HILLS

The hills of home I understand;
I know what paths to take;
Their slopes are gentle and demand
No map from top to lake.

But from the rim of my small world
    Those far hills beckon me;
Smoke and adventure buck and swirl
    In dark deep mystery.

Their summits tall build dark'ning mass
    Where wild winds roar and crash;
Below, dark storms stalk deep crevasse
    And forked lightnings flash.
Oh, those far hills are mountain size,
    With shadows tall as night;
But other times the giant lies
    All peaceable and quiet.

Some distant day I'll break away
    And make myself to go,
Venturing up that smoky way
    With falt'ring step and slow.
I'll make a path up, up to top
    Where valley meets blue sky;
I'll hail a little cloud and stop
    To rest a spell close by.
I'll hold my breath to force my will
    And step right through today;
Out there, perhaps on that far hill,
    I'll lay me down to stay.

PLANNED

When primal moons moved swiftly by
    And dark corralled the stars;
When fiery comets streaked the sky
    In fatal fetal wars;
When worlds were young and our small earth
    Was still a fiery ball,
Creation could have gone still birth,
    Or maybe not at all.

God moved in Time.
                         He juggled moons,
       Separated oceans,
Set mountains tall to block monsoons,
       Weather-made earth's motions.
The great Big Bang that woke our souls
       And still is streaking out
Channeled us not to huge Black Holes—
       For God's hand moved about
In balance and with super speed;
       Carefully He spaced us
In just the orbit we would need—
       God never meant to waste us.

CLIMBING THE MOUNTAIN HOME

One more ridge and we reach the mountain's crest
       Just as the sun sinks low;
We watch the master Painter paint his West
       With sun's last fading glow.

Then out through the trees shines our little light
       To find us in the gloom;
Content we take, in the cool of the night,
       Slow careful steps to home.

THE END OF A PATH

Confident young trees slimmed the thicket
where summer had spread her green.
The hesitant path penetrated a little way,
then was swallowed all in a step,
as if those who had made it
turned suddenly and fled to their cars
parked along this familiar road.

Beyond the end of the path
lay a small cove
with its bubbley spring.
Here we spread our lunch,
owning like masters of all we surveyed
the cloud-patched sky above us
supported by tall birch.

Sun dimmed to twilight;
evening turned a deeper Smoky Mountain Blue;
day hung teetering on the edge of the night,
and we were only two
quickened hearts in a green-tunneled universe
as we watched the early stars pinwheel above our trees.

DIAMOND-BACK ON SOCO

Animal fear flares my nostrils;
It sticks, thick-coated, to my tongue.
I cannot hold the pounding of my heart, shake loose the
      taste, nor dislodge this choking that rises in my throat.

Still now, still as death.
Oh, what simile I have dragged from reason for the mind!
Here! There! Beside me!
The deadly hellish *whir-r-r*
Comes striking up from all around me.

Each blurring, whirling instant dissolves more marrow of
      my quick-softened bones,
Leaving the husk of me.
I cannot see
This whirring dervish of hell's own infernal bell-ringing;
Ringing just for me!

In blessed frozen indecision I cling to my paralysis.
I must hold immobile through this eternity of hell. . . .

Now quiet, but for the frenzied pounding, this pulsing in
    my temples.
There is no ringing, no whir.

Returning courage strokes down the rising hackles of
    my fear-crazed mind;
Slowly, ever so carefully, I retrace my steps.
Another day, another path I'll find.

JUST AN IDEA

Rainbows look best sometimes through tears;
    Often it takes heartache
To guide Hope surely through our fears,
    A stronger life to make.
So, times I'm sure it must be wrong—
    This heav'n folks have painted—
No challenge there, for all is song;
    Everyone is sainted.

No one can stray from golden streets,
    Harps and hallelujahs,
Or find small meadows where one meets
    Bloomin' Howdedudahs.
It's all eat cake; there's no cornbread;
    All is praise, no working;
There's no deep swimming hold to tread,
    And no call to shirking.

So how do rainbows find their tears?
    And sunsets get earth-dust?
How do they nurture Hope with fears?
    Of choose when choose they must?
Please, God, just one meadow surely
    For boys and girls to find,
With fishes swimming, just purely
    As challenge to the mind.
I do admit I don't know much;

It's just I'm assumin'
With all those golden streets and such
    Some small lonely human
Could feel refreshed and soul renewed
    In worship as he romped
Across tall meadows freshly dewed
    Where each bare foot had stomped.

And in one corner, just for looks
    In case there's too much noise,
Please, God, leave some hidden nooks
    With woodsheds, just for boys!

CITY BOY IN THE SMOKIES—

CEREBRUM, CEREBELLUM AND MEDULLA OBLONGATA

The little thought leaped up, hell-bent;
From Cerebrum, wildly it went
Streaking by Pons Varolia
Through Cerebellum's euforia.

Like Paul Revere's wild, wild late ride,
And passing everything, it cried,
"O Medulla Oblongata,
Quickly, Sir! There's been a lot a
Things come up that now we must do,
And we are counting, Sir, on you!
Arouse the heart; we face disaster;
Alert the lungs—faster, faster!
Tell Cerebellum to break through
And move those fat legs!
                            Quickly too!
For some things there are no matches!
You'll soon know if this clown catches
                            You!
Hey! Slow-poke son-of-a-gun!
You think that Smoky Bear can't run?"

GRANDFATHER MOUNTAIN

Millions of years ago tall waves forced primal sea's slow
    parting;
Framed there in spray Grandfather's face up from the deep
    was starting.
Before most mountains could be shorn from off the breast of
    ocean,
While whole continents lay unborn, land creatures but God's
    notion,
Grandfather first, then one by one they lofted up to stations,
These Blacks, Blue Ridges, Great Smokies—our Southern
Appalachians.

Grandfather, we salute you now, great elder of us all;
Hundreds of miles removed from sea, more hundreds
    fathoms tall!
Oh, Geology explains well the you that we've been seeing;
Each huge rock, ev'ry crevice, when with you I'm being.
But what a mystic kinship comes back from you to me!
Sad and lonely, I recall that same wild, primal sea.

Could God have walked those waters then, striding from peak
    to peak,
Falconing my fledgling soul, strange mutiny to seek?
Somewhere over the Black Mountains, winging wild, flying
    free,
Could swift as hawk my willful soul be now eluding me?

Only emptiness I feel instead of Soul in place—
A loneliness, an incomplete, a form without face;
Eyes and arms and feet, floating somewhere alone;
A clock on a steeple that has no hands, making Time
    unknown.

I must get back my errant soul!
                         Grandfather, help me to find!

I must offer Soul in atonement, to gain peace of mind.
O let me have it back, Grandfather, from you or from the sea.
Soul must return to its Falconer if I'm to ransom me.

And what if perhaps this mystery of where my Soul may be
Is clear to God the Falconer, and to you, but not to me?
Then I ask you this, Grandfather: On Time would God have
    tripped
And my soul flung free from His long strong arm somehow
    have slipped
Through the scarred, crevassed bosom of you, deep lodged
    near your heart?
If so, I cannot dig Soul out; I'll never even start!
Pray waste me not, flung off in Time, lost in aeons of weeping;
Let me stay me close, and confident; Soul safe in your
    keeping.

CLIFFS OF DESTINY

Mountains proclaim Eternity.
    In chiseled stone across earth's face,
    Stencilled in cloud, mirrored by space,
    Their sun-crowned glory locked in place—
These mountains call to me.

In roaring canyon filled with spray
    My soul cries out from awful depths;
    Steep fossiled walls belay my steps;
    Soulless I climb, and fear accepts
My challenge of this day.

On to the heights that beckon me
    I climb and cling with numb, bruised feet;
    My spirit on those heights will meet
    The soaring hawk, not shall defeat
Decide my destiny.

MOUNTAIN AIRPORT

Here towered once the lofty hill,
    Inset with fern, tall-pined,
With sinewed rock and gristled root
    Through hard red clay; then vined
Across the face in tangle tight
    All things that God grows green—
Who here on this forsaken cliff
    Should ever have foreseen
More than the nesting of some bird
    In spring; or come that fall
Perhaps a pheasant or a hawk
    On lonely winds that call?

But roar on, O Tuckaseegee,
    Roar on, you island-bound;
And lift your heads, you Smokies,
    You Smokies all around;
For now your cliff lifts proudly up
    Her new face to your sky;
Seductive, wanton, calling down
    All those who once flew high
Above, beyond the ruggedness
    Of these great lovely hills—
And through man's small but willful mind
    His destiny fulfills.

Now shadow swiftly paces thought
    Across earth's trackless face,
And where stood once God's tall green cliff
    Man has smoothed a place
To send his brave in thunder forth,
    His timid souls to nest;
Here where the tall earth meets the sky
    Man comes down to rest.

DITCHING

A ditch is a simple thing, they say.
Nature makes them.
Every day
I see some rivulet or rill
Whose moss-bound rocks glisten still
From soft caress of water's feet
Tripping along, gone to meet
Its river.

After the shower I have stood
In this calm, nature-shapen wood.
The moss, unruffled, glistened still
In crystal depth of shallow rill;
And only a trickle, a soft *drip, drip,*
Went seeking the creek
For its river trip.

Once I decided to make a ditch,
If what I made you'd call one.
I carved the thing straight down a hill,
A simple ditch, a small one.

And when the shower called to me
I hurried to my hill,
But most of it had gone away
To roil the crystal rill.

Yes, a ditch is a simple thing, in a way.
So thought I too until that day.

Now I know better.

So if to dig you get the itch,
Here are some facts about a ditch:

Too much grade, your ditch's snout
Is a pancake-eating pig;

Too little, your ditch will sulk and silt,
And neither run nor dig.

Two ways there are to make a ditch.
By far the most appealing
Is, of course, nature's way,
Cutting, shaping, healing.

The other is for engineer,
Careful, scientific.
Other ways, a ditch can be
Frighteningly terrific.

DANIEL BOONE

The Yadkin farm held little charm;
    Boone craved once more his rude,
Lonely living as backwoodsman
    In some far solitude.
And so—the yellow Yadkin
    Went lazily to sea;
While Boone looked boldly Westward
    Where whisperings seemed to be.

In the dawn Boone walked softly
    Along the Yadkin's bank;
By noon the sluggish river
    Lay far behind him; now he drank
Of crystal-clear spring water
    That ran with merry trill
Hard by his well-hidden fire
    Beneath a wooded hill.

The lurking Cherokee there spied
His twinkling fox-fire camp,
    But with the dawn
    Dan Boone had gone.

The redskin heard no tramp
Of stealthy step on forest floor,
And found no trail; for evermore
This wary paleface covered track,
Now pressed forward, now cut back
Through deeper forest glades
    Where the brown bear kept his den,
Till only the young deer's nimble feet
    Followed where he had been.

Four days Boone traveled, sun till sun,
    Heading over West.
Late on the fifth his climb was done.
    He stood now on the crest
Of a stately peak; the blue of the sky
    Dropped low through the crotch of a ridge,
And mountain men rose, row on row,
    To pillar a cloud-arched bridge.
Two sentinel peaks stood hard North
    And a valley sprawled below;
Here a summer's wind made merry sport,
    And the buck with his maiden doe
Came down at twilight oft to drink
    From out this trinkling fountain
That threaded many a chestnut grove
    From its springhead on Rich Mountain.

Boone pitched his camp beside this spot
    Where first he stooped and drank;
He made his bed by a chestnut's trunk,
    Close to the brook's West bank.

II

Faint streaks of dawn were still in thrall
    Beyond the ragged Brushies,
And chestnut branches still held all
    Their orioles and thrushes;

But Daniel Boone beside this brook
  Long since had left his nap;
Again to West he turned to look
  Beyond the low ridge gap.

The sun came up. He stood and gazed
  Till Yadkin lost all charm.
His vision grew: sleek cattle grazed
  And here and there a farm
Began to dot this virgin land,
  His new-found Paradise;
Pioneers made new demand—
  And through the traveled eyes
Of this man Boone in sixty eight,
  Who loved to live alone,
This rich valley read its fate.
  For Boone at once had known
That not for long could Solitude
  Make here her still abode;
Soon for him would be once more
  Only a Westward road.

III

It's many a year now come and gone
  Since Daniel Boone there camped;
Many the does have brought forth fawn
  And through this valley tramped.
But still Boone's brook murmurs beneath
  Rich Mountain's stalwart brow;
Still summer breezes weave their wreath
  Of cloud gems o'er it. Now
Near Cove Creek is built this town,
Where winding streets lead up and down
  To ferret out the stores;
Or twine about the mountain's lap
  To people's yards and doors.

Along the brook on either side
College portals open wide
    To youngsters still exploring;
But few among them know that Boone
    Here treasure still is storing.
Only the mountains stand to guard
    Lest harm should him befall,
While all his hills join hands as ward
    Against some savage; all
Up and down long village streets
    Boone's valley have crisscrossed;
And far above the cloud-folk play;
    Like sheep from shepherd lost,
They race down steep old Howard's Knob
    To fold in ribbons of mist
The whole of the valley—
    Where once a maiden kissed
Strings of gaudy English beads
    Brought home by her own true brave
And hidden here, known but to her
    And the dead in his shallow grave.
Snugly still in its village cloak
    Boone's valley sprawls at ease
Beneath Rich Mountain and Howard's Knob
    And groves of chestnut trees.
But in the night when phantom moons
    Come pirating through the clouds,
And the chestnuts sway in ghostly dance
    Like rustling spirit shrouds:
Buckskin clad, and with moccasined feet,
    Like some Cherokee spirit
Boone stalks again by his shallow brook,
Or pitches camp in some sheltered nook
    Close by, where he may hear it.

IV

Even today, the stories go,
    Rich Mountain's tree-lined tresses

Shake soft snow to the valley below
　And the Wind will say, "Three guesses!
Find the grave of this mad-mad Boone!"
　But the snow-bound little Village
Replies in one deep chilling breath,
　"He sleeps; he sleeps here, with his pillage!"

Then old Rich Mountain shakes his head
　And frowns down through the valley,
While out from the rocks that crown his brow
　there rumbles forth this sally:
"Pennsylvania gave him birth,
　This Boone, our foster son;
Kentucky and Missouri claimed his dust
　When his work here had been done."
Now Howard's Knob blows rattling breath
　Down through the shadowed town,
Nodding his shock of granite gray
　Until there tumbles down
A loosened stone from his shaggy brow.
It rolls on through the blizzard;
　Scarce heard above the squally blow,
　It crashes in a deluge of snow
As if to mark Boone's grave. Still is heard
The quarreling voice of the mountain men;
　One to another is talking;
While dimly seen, to the lea of the Knob,
　The buckskin figure comes stalking.

V

A tomahawk swings from his leather belt,
　A powder horn hangs to his side;
　His jaw is firm; his measured stride
Is swift but silent; there is felt
The bulging muscle of this man
　In a single glance of eye;
Hangs from his belt a long keen knife,
　A shot pouch by his thigh.

Around his shoulder runs a thong
      Of buckskin; at its end is found
His rifle, whose sudden bloody song
Cursed many a Cherokee brave
and once a warring Shawnee:
      There pausing to drink
      At the Watauga's brink
In the chill of the early dawn he
Had painted his face with berries red
And thirsting for sight of pale faces dead,
Left the Watauga, skirted the Toe,
      And with all his savage hate
Searched the Yonahlosse below
      Where he knew his foe must wait.
Now the buckskin figure glides
      Low through the shadows, keeping
Always close to the mountain sides;
      Ever cautiously peeping
To left, to right, as if afraid
      This lurking brave is left
To scalp him now in grassy glade
      Beneath the Knob's deep cleft.

The town is gone, the college, all;
      There's only this lone scout.
A lowered cloud now hides his place;
The chiseled granite of his face
      Sets fancied foes to rout.
Beside the brook he pauses now,
Then melts into his marker's brow.
And still above the wild night's cries
These mountain voices wailing rise
      In long dispute of Boone.
      Then soon—
Ah, yes, it's much too soon—
There shines again the thin-faced moon,
      While spirit watches keep;
'Tis four o'clock this winter's night,

'Tis just before the dawn's pale light,
    The mountains sink to sleep.

VI

So ends our story, all too soon,
Of Yadkin and Kentucky's Boone.
But ask Rich Mountain, Howard's Knob,
    Ask even Tater Hill!
They know full well, as even I,
    That Boone in spirit still
Believes earth's choicest spot to be
    Not Yadkin or Kentucky,
But this rich valley that he found
    That morning when with luck he
Watched sunrise from Tater Hill
    And visioned land that soon
Would raise Cove Creek, Valle Crucis,
    And his town of Boone.

FRIENDS IN BOONE

When the fingers of night tenderly close
    And the valley comes alight
With the scattered lamps of all of those
    Who bravely fight the night;
When Howard's Knob like Atlas stands
    To shoulder his burden of sky,
I cast aside the day's demands
    And seek a cottage nigh.

Passersby would give it no glance,
    The busy world maybe would frown;
Indeed, I discovered it quite by chance,
    With its brick of weathered brown.
But my steps ne'er fail to quicken at sight

Of its winding street, for I know
The welcome of those in whom I delight
  By the warmth of the fireside glow.

So oft when the night steals softly down
  Like a first act curtain, and day
Takes to her slumber, this cottage brown
  Invites me, bids me stay.
The winged minutes turn quickly to hours,
  While fire in the grate burns low;
But still we talk, the love that is ours
  Blazing bright in its friendly glow.

Then once again I'm alone in the night
  Walking home down a winding street;
The village now sleeps; a lone street light
  Keeps watch; the thud of my feet
Resounds afar in the chill night air;
  Hollow echoes race through the town;
But still I'm cozy and warm and sweet
  With friends in this cottage brown.
Not always, for me, this college town;
  Sometimes I shall be far away
When the fingers of night close softly down
  To strangle the sounds of the day.
But a path in my heart will always be;
  For at evening I must down
Through twilight shadows this winding street
  In a far-off mountain town.

GO-GETTER

They tell us that the bumblebee
  In theory cannot fly;
His wingspread for his fuselage
  Just isn't worth the try.
But having asked no scientist,
  Or gone to logic schools,

This lowly bee just spreads his wings
    And does away with rules.

And so in life those mortals who
    Sit tight for Fate to bring
All wrapped and tied with silver bows
    A genuine sure thing
Find while they wait for every piece
    Of Destiny to fit,
Another risks to win the prize
    And walks right off with it.

Tender moments

HAVE NO REGRET

Life's great moments come to us all.
Some we ignore, others walk tall
And stay close by for all our years,
Giving new hope, drying old tears,
Lending us courage to recall
Early dragons and slay them all.

Tender moments, like well-worn gloves,
Warm the heart from long-ago loves,
Give new strength and peace of mind why
We're on the road less traveled by.
Nor should we once ask, want to know
Where that road not taken would go.

AIMLESS RHYME

In sips of lover's laughter, light tripping through the mist,
You vowed to love me ever after; you promised as we
    kissed.

But rainbows end behind strange hills; fickle is the cat;
The gods grind surely in their mills; and that is that.

BESIDE A TENDER TREE

Many a path ago
Beside a tender tree
Spring gave her strange magic to night's soft glow,
And you were there with me.
The world drew back in shadow
And you were mine, all mine.

But moons burn low
And sink away;
The bitter sweetness I have come to know
Is all my treasure. Who can say
How long is a shadow?
How far is a path?
When tall grows the slender pine.

I JUST STOOD THERE, LOOKING DOWN

Holding hands as lovers will,
We had climbed old Sharpe Top Hill.
Then you sat, your back to me.
Turned away, you could not see
How I felt that summer's day
While you made the daisies say
Who would be your lover true and tried.

Oh, I could just have gone and died,
It broke my heart, I could have cried.

We had more daisies. Don't you see?
You could have counted out on me,
But you didn't, didn't do it—
While the little pale-eyed bluet
Crumpled, bleeding, under nervous feet.

It was fitting, it was meet,
That you tease me, not entreat;
It's part and heart of woman, ever bound—

I know now, but I could not then,
For I was nine and you were ten
And no more bashful lover could be found.

PROGRESS SOMETIMES IS SAD

Would she, blushing, have turned away
From hanging clothes that summer's day
If, woman-like, beneath clothes line
She could have read those thoughts of mine?
I think not, really. For, you see,
Her lovely form made poetry
Of every motion, goodness knows,
A girl should use in hanging clothes.

I'm glad her father's fence was low;
I'm pleased she hung her clothes just so.
And lest you question my good sense,
Or rush to raise her father's fence,
I long ago made book for life—
I took the girl to be my wife!

Nor did jealousy build fence higher—
I bought her an electric dryer!

Now evenings as I latch our gate,
I pause, sadly to contemplate
Frustrations of today's young Joes
Who, thanks to science, see no clothes
Intimate, sequenced on a line,
Nor find the girl as I found mine.

IN JOYCE KILMER FOREST

Eight hundred yards, the marker showed,
Of winding, woodsy little road
That wound about through forest glade,

Uphill and down, until it made
One last sharp turn.
                    Then up it climbed,
Its tree-lined steps as couplets rhymed,
Till dank and darkness fell away
Before thin slits of blue-lit day.

I reached the plaque, and as I read,
How still the forest!
                  How the dead
With living presence filled this wood
In quiet peace.
             Then as I stood
A soft low whisper trilled the trees.
A small wind came and joined the breeze.

The breeze, the wind, now soft with care,
Caressed the forest, lingered there;
While back and forth the tall giants swayed
With quiet rhythm.
             As they prayed
I would have gone, but soul still stood
With bared head bowed in Kilmer wood.

SHORT WALK

This tempting fluffy shadow crossed our path that day;
Its leafy welcome coolness whispered to us to stay.
Here while away your afternoon in peace and idleness;
Let tangled nerves stretch out a bit, forget the daily stress.

It proved too much; we stopped and sat, Time's minutes
    ticking out;
A busy Ant stopped by to chat, then yawned and crept about!
It seemed that God had placed us there, just so beside His way,
Then upped the heat a notch or two so we would choose to
    stay.

43

It was perfect to sit a spell, even an afternoon,
And when we left the sun was low; the day had gone too soon.
We chose our same walkway to home and fitted key to lock,
Regaling in the walk we'd had (actually one short block).

We'd started out to see the lake and watch the duckies swim,
Then have the new mare run the fence, head high, all sleek
 and trim.
We knew we needed exercise and walking was our way;
We'd had no notion just to sit and idle one half day.

But somehow peace and naught to do had smoothed taut
 nerves full out.
The busy Ant who'd stopped to chat was fast asleep, the Lout!

The shade and you were all I knew that one short afternoon.
What can I say?
                    A perfect day!
                              Let's go again!
                                        And soon!

PLEASE

Make for me a melody,
    Sing to me some song;
Cross your fingers, make a wish,
    Help my day along.

Shape a smile and toss to me
    As you pass my tent;
Surround me with your laughter
    And I shall be content.

MOUNTAIN MAY-DAY

Mountains have stood millions of years
    And shall be standing more

44

When we have bowed beneath Life's fears
    And found another shore.
Flowers then will bloom as sweetly,
    With fragrance just as gay,
As when just now you came to meet me
    On this first day of May.

Still lay our valley in her new
    And lovely dress of spring;
How very wonderful were you,
    And how the bells did ring!
So never shall a brighter sun
    Shine down upon a day
That holds more joy than has this one
    For one sweet hour in May.

And never shall God's hand caress,
    Polish hills more newly,
Or they give out such happiness
    As hearts who love truly.

MOUNTAIN FALL

Gay foliage fills these thousand hills
    With richest red and brown;
Bright golds and yellows fit for kings
    Are over all the town.

No winding way but now will lead
    To new majestic views,
Where yet more mountains lie fresh dipped
    In long-lost rainbow hues.

For truly God our Smokies gave
    First choice in richest color,
Leaving all who later chose
    A choice much the duller.

REVERIE

Fall is here and everywhere
    Dry leaves come tumbling down;
An iciness hangs in the air
    As over all the town
Sweet summer has departed us,
    Replacing its bright sheen
With darker browns and somber golds
    Along the village green.

Sad I should be, but still I have
    Sweet memories of spring
To last me into winter and
    The chill it's sure to bring.

You are my Spring, personified,
    And all spring means to me.
Some gracious god just sent you down
    To keep me company.
So I shall always think it's spring
    When you are by my side;
And with the warmth and love you bring
    I shall be satisfied.

FANTASY IN THE SHOPS

All through the aisles
we picked and chose;
you took these,
I wanted those;
but, oh, no,
goodness knows,

        we never argued, did we?

I pushed the cart,
you filled it up,

but runneth over
was my cup!
you let me talk,
then went ahead;
it didn't matter what I'd said—
                    we never argued, did we?

Department store
or porno shop,
we went right on,
we did not stop,
but on and on,
'til needing rest
we turned back home
and that was best!
we never argued, did we?

Oh, you to me were heaven-sent,
so on we went and went and went,
'til neither knew just what it meant—
                    but we never argued, did we?

PILLOW TALK

Our quarrels were never enough, somehow,
    To change the patterned years;
For love is made of sterner stuff, I vow,
    Than these few tears.

In light caress or midnight tryst, I see
    Your beauty ever young;
And each time, Dear, that we have kissed, to me
    New lyrics Love has sung.

Tonight an old remembered fire, like wine
    Hot simmered, stirs my head.
What need of love's mundane attire, or thine,
    When sleep has fled?

SOMETIMES

I put you on a pedestal;
    I think you're super great;
But then straightway I pull you down
    To be my earthy mate.

I float you off on soft Cloud Nine,
    My Princess, virgin, pure;
Then selfishly I make you mine;
    I own you and I'm sure

That sometimes you might rather be
    More independent; and
When I shall fade away a bit
    I'll try to understand.

FANTASY IN MARCH

It was one of those dreary days in early March.
Not at all like one I would order, but then
The Man doesn't drop around to take an order
For my kind of day very often, good or bad.
    This one had been hurry, hurry . . . No,
    Nothing this time, thank you . . . .
    Sorry, not just now . . . Maybe later . . . .
Hour after hour, ads, promotions, cons,
And any other thing being peddled that day.

Then sun shone through and she stood there,
Like a March breeze, like warm spring air.
I wanted to say, What took you so long?
I could not speak. Her siren song
Sang *Goodbye Winter.* Her long flowing hair
I wanted to touch, but I didn't dare!
As in a trance, I just sat there.

Besides, you don't contain a Spring Spirit. Frighten her
As she lingered so beautifully
And she would be gone, I knew.
So I went to lunch. Rather early for lunch and
I wasn't hungry. Part of me stayed by my window,
Eager to reach out; to renew spirits with her;
To offer mine in some awkward annual ritual of exchange.

    I wanted to beg, please don't run away;
    Rest here, Free Spirit; all year you must stay.
    And at such point in time one does not press
    For *No, Maybe,* even hopefully, *Yes.*

I dreamed of tropics and wild red sunsets;
Of fishing from banks of tall thick grass.
I wanted to lay my head softly into her lap,
Or skinny-dip later in some far lagoon.
But you don't just do these things; not yet, perhaps never.
Such Spirits are rare;
    again I must tell you, they are not possessed,
    contained, forced to formula, format, or
    any other way we think we should do these things.
To clutch the wild bird that has flown against your window
And for the moment, stunned, lies at your feet
Is too often the order for total destruction.

    But know, Spring Spirit, I really do care.
    Let me eat those long lunches, dream of your hair;
    Then I'll go back to work, refreshed and meek—
    Just grant me spring fever this one last week.

WHEN YOU CALL

It always helps to have you call. . . .
When I am far away. . . .
Even if it's just "Hello, and how are you today?". . . .
Somehow you have a magic sound. . . .

Even, soft and sweet. . . .
I can imagine that it says. . . .
"Soon, ah, soon we'll meet!". . . .
And I can feel, oh, super good each time I hear you say. . . .
Those same words, so soft and clear. . . .
"I've missed you today!"

AFTER WORK

I found this penny in the street
   Once back upon a time,
But times have changed, and just today
   I found a bright new dime.
It felt so light.
           When I looked close
The silver wasn't there;
But from my mirror just by chance
   I saw it in my hair.

Inflation, too, has taken hold
   To bow me down beneath,
And gold has gone so out of reach,
   It's only in my teeth.
But one thing I find still unchanged—
   From it I will not part!
When every other thing has gone,
   You'll still be in my heart!

THANKS

I'm very grateful to you, dear,
   For clearly you must see
The many things I never am,
   Yet always meant to be.
Your understanding covers well
   My too-loud, splashy ties;

Patiently you let me tell
    Tall tales that otherwise

I'm sure would never interest you,
    But still you smile so gay
And let my ego run its course
    With silly things I say.
So I am grateful, though I know
    I'll always be just six,
Doing handsprings on your lawn,
    A show-off, doing tricks

Like some Tom Sawyer or Huck Finn
    Whose pride in bandaged toe
Asks approval from you or
    Your sympathy, and so
I'm grateful that you understand
    When too much I annoy
That though in years I've grown a man,
    At heart I'm still a boy.

THANK YOU!

I have no mail man! None the less
    I always get my mail!
It's in my box or on my porch
    Each morning without fail.

I have no wish to change this plan;
    Strictly, it no one's biz!
You see, my Mailman is a girl—
    We'll leave that just as is!

And since Yuletide's so far away,
    And fast I grow older,
I send her now this gentle wish:
    Thanks, Dear!   (There! I told her!)

BROKEN MIRROR

In your laughing eyes
Paradise
Was for me.
Now I see.

The last act curtain you may draw.
Those worlds I saw
Through strangely kindled fires
Were but my own desires
Peeking right through
The soul of you.
Misled by laughing eyes,
I only thought the Paradise
Lay there, gleaming new.

I wince now to hear your name.
I see now the cold dull frame.

YOU

My life seems made to order for
    Those moments you are in it;
My heart keeps begging for your love,
    I cannot lose one minute.

For all my days and nights are filled
    With you when I'm away,
And all my loneliness finds peace
    When once again you say

"I'm awfully glad you're back, my dear;
    The week has been so long."

Oh, could you hear how loud my heart
    Sings back its welcome song!

Please, my darling, keep me so,
    Just tailor-made for you,
And wear me snugly, wear me well,
    Life's fleeting season through.

And if perchance in later years
    Forever we're apart,
Let yet the other dwell as now
    Deep in a loving heart.

REMEMBERING

I remember the night I first saw you,
    A little apart from the crowd.
I remember so well—
                    Oh, yes!
                            I do!
You floated me off on a cloud.

I took with me the look I had managed,
    Quite surprised I guess I would say,
For the image of you walked home with me
    And lingered on day after day.

I remember our first talk, mostly books,
    Dull, dusting away on some stack;
Then surprise, one small awkward kiss,
    And quickly you gave it back.

These memories are now a part of me.
    I remember, and I want you
To be there as well, caught up in the cloud,
    And dreaming a little bit too.

OH, GOSH!

When you are out and I'm about the business of my day
I think of many, many things to you I want to say.
     When you get home!
Hard I have tried but you beside me seems to tie my tongue;
I'm awkward. I don't understand just how I come unstrung,
     And melt away!
On a summer day I'm chewing gum plugged on a tree!
I'm butter left too long on a stoop. Globby. Yep, that's me!
     Butter nutty me!
I'm a hunk o'cheese left in the sun, melting on a stump;
I'm gooey inside like spoiled ice cream, dumped on some
   dump.
     Old soft putty. Me!

NEW YORK IS A WONDERFUL TOWN

Let's take a walk through Central Park
   While the snow is fresh and new;
Where the lovers stroll hand in hand,
   And always two by two.
Then let's walk down Park Avenue,
   But careful on that ice;
And if the cold is biting you,
   We'll stop.
        It would be nice,
To cross to 7th.
        Stop once more
And chocolate for two;
Then back we go, back to home
   Where all my world is you.

MOST OF ALL

You touch me
    and I lean into your touch
    as a tired man
    props to a wall.

You hold me
    and I do not feel so much
    suspended
    ready to fall.

I think of you
    and I'm all alone
    on a dark ocean
    awaiting your call.

I love you
    and the heavens thunder
    as we snuggle under
    complete oblivion.

I love that most of all.

ETERNITY, A DEFINITION

Yes, I know Eternity though I haven't been there yet—
It's line on line of lonely years before we ever met.

It's waiting out there, double-parked, while groceries you
bring;
It's standing anxious in the dark and letting your phone ring.

And, no, Eternity is not when we talk on the phone;
Before I move from that one spot an hour has up and flown.

Nor is it when we're lying close, and merging, one from two—
Eternity will forever be when I am there with you!

FULL MEASURE

Whoever, my dear, is ever to know
    The Jekyll and Hyde that's in us;
The purring kitten that we come to know
    Ends up the jackal to skin us.

But so goes life, and its hindsight gained
    Will seldom stop our blundering;
The owl and the cat, now asleep in the tree,
    By night go prowling, plundering.

The full measure is, one friend to one friend,
    Keep warm our deep understanding;
For each must give, give in order to live—
    Giving *more* is *less* demanding.

The full measure is, one friend to one friend,
    Give, give as our love allows us;
For the more we give, the more we do live
    And our hate much less devours us!

CLOSENESS

Your existence wraps itself about me like a summer vine.
my being is devoured.
I become a vessel of spiced and fiery wine;
I'm overpowered
with your lusty, searching hunger for me.
as the earth receives warm rain
I bend to you, a lone slender tree
that lightning strikes to pain.

Please take of me and feed on me
as morning thrives on dew;
when the evening comes and I'm gone home,
I'll live on, part of you.

SERENADE

my heart keeps singing to you
in some sort of crazy off-beat time . . . .
far off in the twilight
a soft guitar keeps strumming
under gypsy skies.

I keep thinking, things to do . . . .
but my head stuffs up with silly rhyme
like the awkward schoolboy I'm quite
capable of becoming
when I look into your eyes.

A PRESCIENCE OF YOU

Alone in a crowd with thousands of faces
               I see only you.
question not the why of it all.
                   I recall
only the softness of your voice purling words to me
with wonderfully soft Christmasy sounds newly formed;
thousands of warm-knit shawls
sheltering me through the long winter's snow.

I feel the light touch of you against my knee;
you sense the quickening motion of me
as I go heart-skipping with you
over paths of the mind in kindling exuberance
alive with a strange prescience just of you and me.

Kiss me lightly, lightly through your tears,
or laugh and yet you make it so,
for in that cosmic flow
of the you and the me that we have come to know
will dwell our world, our years.

LINES

With love
I fashioned a garment
of many shadings, minds and moods;
you wear it well.

YESTERDAY WAS VALENTINE'S DAY

And I thought about you most of the day,
But I didn't know quite what I should say.
Now, this day after, I've come to regret
Not sending the card that you did not get!

AND THAT'S THE WAY IT IS!

Despite logic, rule out reason,
Love will always have its season.
And the *why* is simple.
                        Right from the start
You think with your head; you love with your heart!

BY MY ARITHMETIC

Tonight you will be mine again
back in my arms
and safe.
Tomorrow night?
the same.
But, oh, the eternities
of waiting.
the nights without you
all alone.

I know only that I need
all your love;
I know that I miss you
very much.
I know that love
such as you have given me
when divided into Time
leaves one lifetime
not enough.

LINES

Out of mind and out of space
where moons spin wild and free
let us find some special place
and wait out history.

*HOW DO I LOVE THEE?
LET ME COUNT THE WAYS

I envy the complete possession sleep takes of you.
The little pout that slips out and skittles about
Until I catch it off the corner of your mouth.
The quiet sounds your lips make at whatever it is they do
While you quickly drift away,
A neat tangle of arms, legs and feet
With twin peaks of loveliness just North of South.

So still now you sleep!
Covers aside, unashamedly you lie
Cuddled, twisted, with all of you in view.
It welds anew our Love.
                              You satisfy.
                                        I am content with you.

* *The title is old, and borrowed, too.*
  The subject as fresh as morning dew.

THE CHOICE

to all who wish
    upon a star,
    wherever you are, be not afraid . . . however disarrayed;
    to all who
    are lonely,
incomplete,
star-struck or dreaming
    indiscreet—
    please do
not be dismayed . . . that you have strayed
to the singles-bar syndrome
    only to find
    loneliness
and no real peace.

    be not surprised
    if Soul still searches
to find release.

but if another choice you made;
    if perchance you have stayed . . . steadfast,
    and you are unafraid,
please know:
    fidelity . . . at last
has its sweet reward.

LINES

Come, walk with me through
the supermarkets of life;
let us spend together
what we have to spend.

STRANGERS

You are
        the girl of my thousand dreams,
And yet
        I wonder sometimes.
Have we met?
Could you be my fantasy
And we
Have really never known each other.
flesh to flesh,
        at all!

Oh, you stand tall
When I dream of you,
but I reach to touch,
to say, "I do,"
and only shadows echo back to me.
There is no you to see.

WAITING TO BE FILLED

Days are empty casks
Lined row on row.

Days are as sponges long removed from the sea,
Or as sailors far from port;
They are filled with emptiness,
And long for sweet strong wine.

Days are an eternity of tomorrows
Stretching away to the desolate years.

A THORNY PATH TO ROSES I

SHUCKS!

List all her faults? You listen here,
That might just take sometime next year.
I drive the car, she tells me how;
Just one wee slip, Oh, gosh, Oh, wow!
I've let the cat out of the sack!
I talk too damn much. Yak! Yak! Yak!
I've dropped some chips, I've dribbled coke—
O heaven help—I wear her yoke!

But then sometimes when I am near
She dabs perfume behind her ear
And picks and pecks and coos at me
And I remember perfectly.

DÉJÀ VU

When I think back I'll never know
How I could marry that old Crow.
Young handsome me (know what I mean?)
Why not have picked some Beauty Queen?
That Bachelor Life was such great fun—
'Til, damn, she tricked me, and she won.

BACK TOGETHER

I felt like hell. We were at war.
Now blessed truce. It's best by far
To reason and talk out these things—
I wait to see just what peace brings.

Hope springs eternal, so it's said;
I'll say a prayer and go to bed.

A THORNY PATH TO ROSES II

YUCKS!

He's careless. Oh, it's such a waste
The way he squeezes his toothpaste,
Or cannot find his underwear—
Just seems as if he doesn't care.
He drops his towels in the shower;
I could now spend the next long hour
Listing his faults and how they hurt.
Yes, Dear! I've ironed it. Here's your shirt!

Honest, I know he doesn't care,
But, yes, you guessed it. Dumb old Bear
Could never make it without me.
He'd never find a new Bee Tree—
His Honey Bee!
Another me!
Ge-e-e!

OH, YEAH!

Move over, Rat! That is my space.
Git! Scat! Go! Hide that face.
I ought to shoot you, but instead
This rolling pin can bust your head.
You just won't treat me fair at all.
Split, Splat, Splatter! Oh, my poor wall!

TRUCE

Come, Honey Bug; come back to bed;
I'm sorry, Sug, those things I said . . . .
Smack! Smack! Oo-o-o, there's more to come—
I love you much, you old Dumb, Dumb.

INEXORABLE

Leaves are falling and the sad
    days of Fall take their toll.
Bright October is a mask of color
    with hints of darker winter to come.
Crickets and small creatures
    fight the numbing chill
    in a struggle to live.
Time moves into the jaws of the death season,
    carrying its own avalanche of beauty
    and burial under winter snows.

LOOKING BACK

Remember the funny-faced gourd we found
    Still clinging to its vine;
Remember the path by the garden wall,
    In a world all yours and mine.
We walked along the old woods trail
    And down the pasture lane;
We stopped by the creek's small canebrake
    And cut a fishing cane.

Our pockets were filled with pebbles,
    Faces wet from a misty rain;
Not once we dreamed such happiness
    Would never come again.

But memories fall like cobwebs
    When you sweep your closets clean;
The cluttered shelves of all that's past
    No longer you want seen.
So pictures are gone and letters burned;
Hate hob-nails former trust.
    Who wrote in his journal
    That love is eternal,
Never bit Love's dust.

REMEMBERING

Snow had fallen on the old woods road;
tree trunks were iced along their North side
away from the fading sun.
I came soon to our old birch tree;
it stood with me in the silent snow
as if thinking on more pleasing summer things now done.
an old mare dozed, standing close against the fence.

I remembered our picnics,
summers under the birch,
and I had assumed, knowing you,
life could always be so full.

Shadows grew longer;
the glist'ing snow lit my path back
for winter's sun had gone.

So are you, my darling.
I know,
but I am still drawn as if in magic
to the places where once we were merry
   and carefree
      and giving
         and loving.
long, it seems so long, ago
in a far happier time.

I want to think, God willing, that someday
I'll come to find you, just as before.
but I know that is not true—
What once was ours can never be again.

THE BITTER END

   Crush me in the grinders
   of your razor-sharp mind
   until nothing is left.

But neatly, please.
No splatter.
        No blood.

I will not remain a dissected frog
in a musty Mason jar, formaldehyded and pickled,
poked at and gazed upon,
some half-forgotten remnant of the past.

I could be Ugly Frog
because you, my pretty Princess, did not show.
You just floated away, you know,
back to mainstream and disappeared.
Demurely you floated on that damned singles pad,
sometimes stubborn, oft-times sad—
I no longer recall.
Was the pad medium? Was it small?
Damn it all !
I won't need to remember anymore.

These days I forget
my box number too.
When I remember and fit the key
it is always empty.
You have gone from me,
carried away on that same damned slippery pad.

Was he short, fat, thin or tall?
I don't recall
I know his fame, I forget his name,
This bar Lothario who
seduced you from me.
You see, fortunately,
Mercy's balm comes much enriched
with lanolin and forgetting.

But not always.
My brother once
when we were very young

pickled a Black Widow
in this small pickle jar.
I never ate pickles again.

The other day some Wise One said:
    "Fellow who falls for, or marries,
        a Black Widow
is headed for bushels of trouble.
Strange. Until now
I thought I had pretty well managed
to control my passion for Black Widows."

So tell me,
How do the Young Unknowing
become so smart nowadays?
How do I, Ugly Frog who lost his Princess,
so lately seem so dumb?

Well, life ain't always
to the swift, Br'er Rabbit.
Herpes remains the same toothy old Wolf,
covered right to his ears in Grandmother's bed,
waiting impatiently to grab Little Red.

But sometimes Life doesn't seem unfair.
When departing it can be so very simple,
Should the Gentle linger longer,
or suffer more, in order to die?

AFTERWARDS

I ask you because you will know.
Why does the grass grow over my window?
Who made that new path from the hill?
Where does the cow graze after her milking?
Why is the pond so still?

Who built the new house by the river
    above Horseshoe Bend?
Are the neighbors kind to you?
and church? Do you still attend?

What killed the maple out by the barn?
Is the stallion restless still?
And darkness?
       It comes sudden, with a sharp, quick swoop,
    surprising you over the hill . . .
Tonight the wild dogs are barking, barking.
I suppose they always will.

LAST LINE

My need has pulled me
into the deep well of you
and I thirst no more.

WAITING TO BE FILLED

Days are empty casks
Lined row on row.

Days are as sponges long removed from the sea,
Or as sailors long from port;
They are filled with emptiness,
And long for sweet strong wine.

Days are an eternity of tomorrows
Stretching away to the desolate years.

REALIZATION

If Love be like heaven,
    Full of strange throbbing music
    And a quiet ecstasy of peace,
I think I have loved.

If love be as a thorn,
    Sharp,
        Cruel,
            Gouging,
And with it all no peace—
    Then I know.

FUTILE MOMENT

I shall seek my last pilgrimage
    When there is nothing more
I have asked, given, sought or found
    That is worthy of store.

Out of all sensitivity,
    Up from darkness ahead,
Time will flow out to engulf me—
    I shall be dead.

SUNRISE

Waste not the time a shroud to fit.
For such brief spell I'll be in it
That least of all can matter size.
No thing counts but the new sunrise.

SALLOW YOUNG MAN

This sallow young man wears glasses,
carries an economics book under one arm,
and is getting an education.
Sure. He came from the farm.
Seventeen years of it. *So what!*

Cotton was eight cents a pound
and hayseed free as the air;
he brought some along, to wear in his hair!
As soon as he combs these all away,
he's going back for more; he's found
they scare away
the painted scarecrows that flap and caw,
drolling of sex
in dainty pecks,
of Nature in the raw.

The sallow young man with glasses
and economics book under one arm
came from the farm
and is proud of it.
But he doesn't want to go back.
Not with the government
spending millions for power lines and leaving him out.
If something isn't crooked, it's badly bent;
so he works hard under the bald-headed professor with the
    gout;
he's finding out, more and more, what it's all about.

He won't go back to the farm!
The government makes him kill his pigs
and then for a slice of high-priced meat
swap bushels and bushels of low-priced potatoes he digs;

there's no profit in that.
somebody is a rat, getting fat;
the professor with the gout
keeps telling him about
these weasels getting fat,
and the sorry mess the country is in;
he doesn't have time to guzzle raw gin,
and go to fast parties that last all night.

So he wears glasses, carries an economics book under one
    arm,
and goes through college searching for an education.

CAMPUS SHOT

The checkerboard of tennis courts
where pale young men in tight blue shorts
pounce on bouncing balls.
Not far away, three stories high,
where classrooms reach to meet the sky,
a professor has opened his window,
high up, on the third floor;
the young men in blue shorts
on the tennis courts
look small and far away.

Isn't Education a bore,
muses the Professor;
he's thought so before.

What fun to be chasing balls
and whamming their daylights out,
but at sixty he has the gout,
and a PhD, and four classes;
and scarcely any fun;
while these addle-brained young asses—
look at that fellow run!—

stay out all night and sleep on class;
spend Dad's dough and hope to pass!

Bah! Running like mad on tennis courts;
shuttling about in tight blue shorts
to pounce on bouncing balls!

CO-ED SUZIE

Tramp! Tramp! Along the hall
It's little Suzie College;
she'd shame a battalion, cannon and all;
when Suzie drifts along the hall
you wouldn't notice a freight train.
Her empty head is common knowledge,
so I hardly know how to explain;
but the boys,
when it comes to Suzie,
put up with the noise—
Suzie has something else.

Once, though surely an accident,
Suzie's dress covered both knees;
but it didn't stay there long.
Suzie meant—
and take it how you please,
but don't take Suzie wrong—
her talents were not to be hidden away
under a bushel, as we're wont to say;
so Co-ed Suzie came and went
across the campus firmament,
and educated the masses,
but took none away.
She spent all her classes—
How shall I say?—
Well, making other girls have green eyes.

But Suzie sure showed the world
where she and Marlene Deitrich
scooped the rest of the gals.

Here's to Suzie.

SPRING LADY

I saw her from my window, her long hair pinned
  with jonquil stems,
    And on her cheek the first faint budding of the
      rose.
Wistfully she gazed on my garden, with its dead
  broken limbs,
    Its unsightly litter to hold the winter snows.

Her skirts were full and flowing, and made a music
  in the breeze
    With the rustle of their passing on my lawn,
But when I had leaped the casement, there were
  only barren trees—
    The roses and the jonquils all were gone.

Weeks later all the rubbish I had raked from flower
  beds;
    All the dead and broken limbs were off the trees;
A million little blossoms stood with proud uplifted
  heads
In open house to calling bumble bees.

I saw her once more; She was chasing a breeze
  through my larkspur bed,
    And kissing her wanton laggard with laughing
      lips;
No longer she spurned my garden; she walked its
  length instead
    Fondling each fragrant blossom with her fairy
      finger tips.

PRAYER FOR THE NEW YEAR

Of the coming Year I ask
My task.
Not on terms of Fortune wooing,
But in coin of simple doing.
Not to have it measured me
In baskets greatly, but to see
The worth of each new day at hand,
And earnestly to understand.

Of my God above I pray
A way.
Not to have it shown to me,
And step by step made known to me,
This way that I must go;
But only that a darkening night
Stifle not Hope, shield not the Light
From feeble steps and slow.

Of myself I ask to be
Just me.
Not because I sink below
Or rise above the ebb and flow;
Not because I wish to be
One aloof, a Pharisee;
But because a place is mine,
A niche to fill; a spark divine
That even I have not the right
To extinguish or to blight.
Then show to me, dear God, Thy way;
Make Grace sufficient, day to day;
Let me find sun, may Hope come winging;
Give me a song made just for singing.
Then inasmuch, for me one day,
As some Soul poorer passed my way
And I have shared and asked Him in,
Wilt Thou not, Lord, forgive my sin?

REQUEST

Pray courage and the discipline of peace
To sustain us.
                Let mind in earth's release
   Give rest to soul.
Pray whatever gods above that be
Rest benediction on us softly
   And stay the goal.

Let life be pleasing to touch and to taste;
May moments be precious, with naught to waste
              From Life's great tree.
For ever it's been, forever must
Go ashes to ashes, dust to dust,
          As you and me.

THE GARDEN TAKEN

I clutched naked soul to the bosom of me and tried to hide my
   sin.
Oh, I wanted to flee but the cosmogony surely fenced me in.

Far above the North Star was the eye of God winking bright in
   the dark;
Below was red where the fire-breathing head of the dragon
   made its mark.

Cosmos was all in order, they said.
                But my garden had been taken,
And a sure salvation had gone with it, leaving my soul
   forsaken.

Where now, Cosmos? Cause and effect? Reward? Adam, Eve
   and the Serpent?
I have been taken!
      God, you changed the plan and left me in torment.

SIMPLE SIMON'S PENNY

I found this penny in the street
Lying hidden at my feet.
I thought: *How neat!*
A shimmering, shining brand-new penny at my feet.

Then I pondered: *How did it fall?*
Was someone deaf? Someone too tall
To hear it fall?

Should this penny fall in Rome
It would quickly find a home.
Chubby fingers outside St. Peters,
Hawk-eyed finders, swift-legged streeters
Would snatch it up in Rome.

But I left it in the street,
Corner Central and Kilbourne, soiled, un-neat.
I had other tempting pies to eat.
Today's prices, what would it buy!
I hurried on and let it lie.

Now this troubles me a bit.
Was that penny it?
Could Simple Simon have called its date?
Was inflation too soon? I too late?

If you should see Simon,
Unlikely as that is,
At Central and Kilbourne
The penny is his!

GATE OF LUCIDITY

Gate, you stopped my entrance
    with your massive lock—
    a stalwart who cried

"Wait! If you seek my
Master you must knock,
    and he lives far, far inside."

Faster feet than mine have tried,
    Gate, to catch you
Swinging wide
    at propitious moment,
    your great hinges
Singing in slow time some hymn of old
Decay—which, in truth, is deceit;
    really you say,
"Today my Lord and Master who dwells here
Re-entered his castle;
    he has hidden away
behind this entrance where I stand
Centered in waiting, bound to obey
    when Knight Key mates with its Lock."

Deny me at will, Old Gate; you are
    of time and tide, and a mind perhaps,
I have failed to catch;
Only by seconds I may have missed,
    but except now I knock,
Lonely eternities to be
    may fail to yield your lock.

PLANTER'S ALMANAC

As only God and rich sandy river loam can grow it,
I remember my father's corn.
    All those green rustling soldier-lines
    Of vibrant whispering life set
Dark against the pale moonlight
Of a hot mid-summer night.

I remember you there with me;
We walked through his summer corn,
The stalk heavy with harvest.

Tipped down for giving, the thin moon
Gave yet no hint of its far, moon-guided
Instinct of origin;
No present thought of later return.

We knew only the calendared surety of father's planter wheel,
  With its pocketed gear
  Dropping seed with measured mechanical rhythm
Against the soft ground.

No one had yet told us how to make sterile
If nothing is to grow;
  Born to prepare for harvest,
  We spend our lives in that hope.

The moon that night too soon was spent.
Soft suction of the deep earth tugged about us.
  There, suspended in Time,
  Lost for one moment in a heartbeat of Eternity,
We knew each other
And you named all the stars.

THE SLY OLD DRAGON

The short, the fat, the lean and the tall—
He hounded them down, he ate them all.

His first fat chop was old Shoe Box Sam,
Followed by one Goon Guffey,
Then Corporate Charlie, Peanut Pete
And Millionaire McHuffey.

Soon only the cupboard bare was left;
The rich now were poor; the poor, bereft

Of once fat givvermint plonder,
Begged Santa: Let's barbeque Donder.

Thus, in a coil of ginger and guts,
Pink cadillacs, pistachio nuts,
And one last gorge of feathers and pelf,
The Critter found he had swallowed himself.

OUCH!

I control my grass, my hedges, my trees—
But dandelions grow where they damn well please!

SPACE-AGE REVOLUTION

Each model change something went wronger,
And Jones's new car grew one foot longer.

Soon most garages lost their roomers,
Or pooched out back with winged tumors.

Had the monsters grown scant inches lower,
Jones could've slid his under his floor.

But, to put it more exacter,
Cars could have grown more compacter,

For, contemplating Detroit's horror,
Jones up and bought a foreign car-r!

DEATH WATCH

Last night Death stopped by and knocked,
then seemed to go away—
but not far, not long enough
to count just one more day.

His chill breath and dark caress
moved slowly on the throat
of one whose life had sheltered me;
I thought I heard Death gloat.

The swift pulse, the labored breath,
angry in its attack,
struggled to pump fitful life,
tried to hold Death back.

But Death moved ever closer
until the deed was done;
life drained from this loved one's face,
breath slowed 'til there was none.

Quickly then Death ran, and much
I felt relieved. From clay
had burst a form Death could not touch—
it rose and soared away.

LATE EVENING WALK WHEN IT STARTED TO RAIN

The smell of leaves moldy wet
and toadstools gleaming white;
the dark forest on and on, interminable,
swallowing my footsteps, yet
holding at bay if only for this, another instant,
the lowering hungry night.

Cobwebs sparkle in the path ahead,
rain-glistened and spidowed;
all are swept aside
in the impetuousness of swinging stride

that breaks at last as the spent swimmer gulps for air,
at the edge of a wood.

Down the broom-sedged path edging a fresh-plowed loam;
one leap over the small brook;
with a great stamping of feet on the back stoop,
at last, breathless, I am home!

THE WILLOW AND THE DAM

Willow in ponds,
thickets of willow
up and down the stream;
willow, willow,
green the willow
as Ireland's wildest dream.

But that was yesteryear, before
Authority built the wall
that covered Bushnell, Twenty Mile,
Hazel Creek and all.

Oh, willow gone
my willow green
and sad it is I am;
I would not give the willow
for all of that big dam!

NE'BOR EBB

Ebb lives a mile or so out my way.
Ebb never has very much to say.

Winter, summer, spring or fall
Ebb says, "Tol'able. How're y'all?"

One day when I passed Ebb did say,
"Howdy. Where you goin', dressed up that way?"

"I'm going to the funeral, Ebb. Hiram Hogshed."
Ebb said. "Old Hiram, huh? I swan. Is he ded?"

So Ebb lives on in his tol'able way
By the side of my road, from day to day.

His conversation leaves much to be desired,
But it's never enough to leave me tired.

FACE TO FACE

How high the mountains, O my Soul!
    How winding is my road!
Beyond which summit lies the goal?
    For how long yet the goad?

To toil and climb, to sweat and grieve
    For something vague, unseen—
What yearns within me that I leave
    This valley's pleasant green?

I cannot prove where or when
    Or even *if* Death gives
Somewhere a passage through which men
    Shall meet God where He lives.

But this I know, as mountains bleak
    Allow these stone-bruised feet,
Glory surrounds some distant peak—
    There, one day, we shall meet.

NOTHING MUCH

Some yet are rough
And some are slick,
But narrow, tall,
Long, thin or thick,
Roman, common,
Smooth face or rough,
To say it all—
And quite enough—
A brick is a
Brick is a brick.

There is no warmth
As such; no use
Unless you need
Doubtful excuse
To bash a mate's
contrary head,
Then wrap and heat
And take to bed
For your chilled feet.

Oh, brick get hot
And brick grow cold,
Some yet are new
And some are old;
Some are of clay,
Quite red and raw,
Others are baked
And made with straw.

But brick are brick,
Are Brick that's all—
Until they're laid
In someone's wall.

PROMETHEUS AND CHIRON

I

I am Prometheus, stealer of fire from the selfish gods,
      bringer of gifts to men.
But I, the once proud Titan, can come no more to serve.
Zeus, chief of the gods, in anger has bound me to this rock;
Even now the vulture feeds with cawing, blood-flecked
      beak.

Though daily consumed, their vengeance nightly renews
      me,
And hell white-hot spews in gush of blood from stabbing
      jab in vulture's claw of pain.

Nor more do I serve man.
Though warmed in the flesh from heaven-stolen fire,
A selfish ice of unbrotherhood lies thick about my
      unthawed soul.

Were I more man and less god, unceasing fervent prayer
      might melt it away.
Were I more god and less man, my will should be enough.

But, oh, how shall I cut this self-hardness from a soft
      bleeding heart
If, shackled hand and foot, devoured eternally by this
      vulture, I am disowned, both by men and gods?

II

Peace, my troubled Prometheus.
I am Chiron, the centaur, skilled in medicines to make
      anew the spirit.
Do you not yet know the answer?

Half horse, half man, and owned of neither,
I too have known the anguish of the claw; am torn eternally
    between over-powering strength and the reason-
    tempered mind.

Now I bear a gift to Zeus.
Each in his own way this gift shall make free.

Come, Hercules, and
Slay the flapping, cawing vulture of my selfish fear.
Were I all men this could not pay your debt,
But go, Prometheus, ever free to serve.
Chiron, the centaur, has taken your place.

UNTIL NEXT MONTH

Old pale moon, now thin and shrunken,
    Dragging low in dawn's first light,
What young sailor, mad and drunken,
    Were you out with all last night?

Where now the tide whose heady surge
    Beat shore in race on race?
Why now once more the young whelp's urge
    To lick his mate's quick face?

O Moon, behind thin curtain drawn,
    Dark shadow found you out;
Slink away through the caves of dawn,
    Go make more cheese, and pout!

EVEN FOR GODS

Hector slew Patroclus, only to face
    Mightier swords than his;

Achilles, idol of his race,
    Slew Hector. So it is
That who survives has fleeting gain,
    Nor safe can ever feel—
Achilles, who could not be slain,
    Found death lodged in his heel.

I CANNOT COME TO PLAY

Catgut cries of sheep, bespeaking
excrement smell and impolite
parlor thought; but does the violin
breathing resonantly in Beethoven's
First Symphony, being strung of the sheep,
so advertise itself in six-foot
neon letters? It is of sheep nor
could deny, but all sweet mystery of
life cascades in its melody
nor mentions catgut once.

Does then the so-called modern, butcher-mad,
drag bloated sex cow bellying through
semen-stained beds and crimsoned rape
of sensibilities to prove how deep of
life he drinks or, braggadocio from psycho
couch raping the sweetness of woman
upon his Dionysiac altar
and boasting thrust to very soul,
enter but skin deep?

Vomit stench be on him
and his reader puke.
June bride rhymes not with phallus,
despite him, nor is there melody of
soul communion in mere belly bareness
dragged from cover, paraded
through the cluttered beds
of unmade minds, sharing glut

of passion-sated exhibitionists
who would put soul in stocks and rape
at will this grand old
mother of mankind.

Let moon and June still halo
marriage bed; nor strip my bride
on wedding night for all the street
to lust after like hung dog
on dungheap till the dawn.

We are the proud, though all us passé,
who will not sleep with whores
to high priest ourselves into unholy
union with guttersnipes or queers.

Better to ape poorly a dead songsmith
than to grace the whore's foul bed;
better we find bad melody
though you will banish us, unread,
than to seek impassioned immmortality
in lewdness, child of fire and worm,
all damned for a reader unworthy of pursuit.

DEFINITIVE WORLDS

Worlds, worlds. Circle, circle, wheel on wheel.
We mentioned a few. You may roll your own. Big deal!

First, take the world of the man who has only himself.
 He feeds himself, he clothes himself, buys tobacco,
 keeps warm, and has only himself to be selfish about.

Then there are the strangely interlocked worlds of spinster,
 old maid, and bachelor girl; the first, manless; the
 second, a speaking acquaintance; the third, no
 husband of her own. The spinster's horizon is seldom
 wider than her own hearth, her sister's three children,

and the ever-circling apron strings. An old maid, bless
her, has horizons broad and liberal, including a career
and the arts—excepting, of course, modern painting
and beatnik poetry. Who could call those arts, anyway?
The bachelor girl? All manner of arts, practicing!

Or consider the world of the transcendentalist. He shuts
his eyes and his undesirable world of the moment is
not there. Of any man today, Social Security notwith-
standing, he could live most roof-tight and worry-free,
nor build great barns where weeviled anxieties might
blight his quickened soul. It is with regret that the
Space Age has lost his unique talent.

Today's ulcered pseudo-realist is just the opposite. Life
for him is one horrendous, taxacious, televised, contin-
uing psychoanalyst's nightmare.

Then take the world of the teen-ager. Oops, Daddy-O!
    Take it, please!
Space Age creeps are infesting our sphere. Dig yuh, Man!
Ziggity!
Oh, there are worlds and worlds, Say on, Exekiel.
And each is a wheel in a wheel.
                              Say on.
They spin like plates on a poker-top edge.
                                    Play on, play on.
Big deal!

OH, PLEASE!

Nurse, open my windows; let God's sun in;
Let me see the decor a man's soul is done in.
Give me good fresh air, something to fight for;
Stars and a breeze worth waiting the night for.

I'm weary; I'm sore; I'm beat by a clock
Going *tick-tick*.
                    Would you speak to the Doc?
Heaven knows, Nurse, I have been so willin',
But give me Faith, not more penicillin!

Prescribe for me trees, with soft grass under,
Crickets to sing, and forests to plunder;
Wheel me out to look at the early sun;
Leave me sit and muse until day is done.

Help me, Nurse, to lose this clinical smell—
And please, no more shots, until I am well!

LESSON IN THE WOODS

I called the pool Complacency;
    Still, deep its placid sky;
Serene my face looked up at me
    From low clouds floating by.

The gnarled old oak on Northern bank
    Leaned downward into sun,
The moss below lay cool and dank,
    Quiet as sleeping nun.

But scarce I'd found this magic balm
    Under the oak tree's bend,
When falling leaves disturbed its calm,
    One acorn brought its end.

And from its ending rose no song
    Of courage skyward ringing;
There played no fife, no drummer's bong,
    No melody worth singing.

I found these in the brook, whose hill,
   Rockstrewn, sought to enslave;
The little brook would not hold still,
   And laughter freely gave.

Here rocks and roughness proved of worth
   To keep a brook singing—
From constant struggle with the earth
   Melody kept ringing.

PASS THE BISCUITS, PAPPY 'N LAW

From the *Salts Of The Earth* to the *Upper Crusts,*
From the *Puny Twenties* to the *Thirty-Eight Busts,*
From the *Glamorous Winners* to the *Never Starts,*
This world is divided into several parts.

And some are the *Haves* and some the *Have Nots,*
But all in between there are lots and lots
Of us wedged in there awfully tight,
Being *Nearly Winners,* but never quite!

We find our apple, but the worm has chewed it,
Which is no good unless we had stewed it.
We find our bargain, and so long we had sought it,
But the fellow in front of us has just bought it.

The roan won the race, we bet on the bay;
And there's more of it, more; as when they say
"Oh, such a good face, but not the legs for it,"
Which is like ham when you don't have eggs for it.

This is our luck, our fate fairly begs for it—
If we have the ham, we never find eggs for it!

But if we get eggs, we find no ham for it—
And, if that's fate, we don't care a damn for it!

THE WATCHED POT

Do you know why a woodbox devours more wood
Than ever the wee laddie thought it could?

Do you know, when he's hoeing or pitching hay,
Why the long, long hours will not pass away?

Can you tell why Christmas, though adults may scoff,
When days away is a thousand years off?

Then put Time aside like an uncut book;
Or a moth in a jar; don't ever look.

Busy yourself with the things of the day,
And Time, pretty soon, will have flown away.

Scarcely minutes between woodbox filling,
Sowing the wheat and taking the milling.

Hardly a breath separates Sundays;
The seasons roll by, all filled with Mondays.

Christmas to Christmas is only a think,
And Time, unwatched, has been quick as a wink.

COST ACCOUNTING

The time grows short, so I must write
The income tax big wheel tonight
And tell him just how hard I've tried—
Though bitter fact is not denied
That of the money in the pot
There's little left.
                    Gee whiz!
The higher cost of living got
All mine and most of his!

DOWN HOME

The memory still is warm to me:
This maverick fence-corner apple tree
That stood on our farm far back on a hill.
The fence was down, but the tree was still
Standing proudly, all covered with vine.
It bore a few apples. Oh, how fine
To pause late in fall and search them out.
Looking for apples, I wondered about
The fellow who once had planted that tree;
I wanted to say, "God, thank him for me;
And give me grace to plant a sprout
For a lad back home, just about
Ready to follow; some day he
Will be needing an apple tree."

AMONG HER ANTIQUES

She showed me through her big old house.
   Each something had a date.
Her great-grandfather made this chair
   In eighteen-thirty-eight.

One piece she quietly passed by,
   Not bothering to show.
I asked. She said, "Oh, I bought that
   Just forty years ago."

ONE ORDER, COMING UP

I'll take six mountains timbered tall,
   One grassy meadow nigh;
Complete, one house, one waterfall,
   And one trail leading by;
Hungry trout in the ice-cold stream,
   Fat deer, quail and pheasant;

No taste flies to spoil my dream
    And make life unpleasant.

Sir! My order you cannot take?
    It's just an ad composite?
But, Man, it says right here to make
    My fifty-buck deposit!
I see.
        Then, Sir, your catalog's
        A phony—in cahoots
To sell more tents, old hunting dogs
    And fancy new trail boots.

HOW KELLI MISSED CHRISTMAS

Claus was up tight.
                    You could tell he
Was awful upset
But why'n hell he
Thought to blame little girl Kelli
Has no honor, no, nor glory—
Clause is stuck with a bad story!

If S. Clause had thought at all clearly,
His plan would've been *Drunk, or nearly!*
Or this could make a better tale:
Yes, I smoke pot; I don't inhale!
Censure me good, but, please, no jail!

Claus could've denied his pack was short;
That Kelli's gifts bought him one last snort;
That he'd slopped Christmas all down that bar,
Then tipsied out, hi-jacked the cop's car,
Dropped his short pack, shouting *Go! Go!*
Thinking Rudolph stood there in the snow.

The gifts all gone, Claus was cold and lost,
Alone, knee-deep in the Soco frost!
And Kelli's gifts? Well, Wadda ya think?
He'd traded them all for that last drink.

CRAZY

When opening a jar
I can tell you it's far
   More difficult to land that first pickle.
If you've caught a pink goose,
Then go to turn him loose,
   That first feather you plucked will still tickle.

Your first apple may be free,
Or so it seems to be,
   But maybe you should go and pick your own;
For apples, one a day,
May keep the Doc away,
   But it won't fool the snake!
                       Eve should've known.

She should've killed that snake!
How simple that would make
   This rocky, sin-filled road we now must tread;
But I can understand,
Eve reached to shake his hand
   And, lo! She held that apple, bright and red.

Eve meant to shake *Good-bye,*
But Devil, oh, so sly,
   Turned his hand into an apple on the spot.
Eve barely touched that hand,
So she doesn't understand
   Why apples passed to us will always rot!

THE PRINCE AND HIS GIRL

This is a tall story of mishap and glory,
   And a tale I just have to tell;
There's a Prince and this Girl who grew a stubborn curl,
   And after that nothing went well.

The curl fouled her eyes 'til as you surmise
   She had short words with her wizard.

The very next day (O, Death, go away!)
　　That curl she dreamed she had scissored!

So the winsome Lass grabbed her looking glass.
　　She saw, and she screamed her disgrace.
I'm so unknowing! That damn thing's growing
　　Right in the middle of my face!

Wizard? You'll answer! Why this huge cancer
　　Should hide my lovely blue eyes?
Oh, faddle, fiddle, it's right in the middle!
　　Take it off or all of me dies!

And while she moaned, she fumed and she groaned;
　　And twitched from her head to her toes;
But a wise Horse Fly Fate sent buzzing by
　　Said, Look! What a luv-lu-vy nose!

So, forgetting her woes, She followed that nose
　　And grabbed old Sir Hansome, the Prince;
Not long she tarried, for soon they married
　　And happily have lived there since.

WELL MAYBE

　　Thank you much, but no one knows
　　Much about these U F O's
　　So on this ride you plan to go
　　Count me out if it's U F O.

　　Yet, I wonder. . . .
　　　　　　I don't quite know.
　　If you could make your U F O
　　Roomy enough, in high style,
　　I might go ride, just one mile!
　　If you would drive her really slow,
　　And you could steer her smooth'n low,
　　I just might. . . .
　　　　　　Why, hell, let's go!

MOONWALK

I crawled up Jack's beanstalk,
Long last I reached the moon.
On this first trip
I thought to sip
From some far deep lagoon.
I fast climbed back—
My new napsack
Did not contain a spoon!
On my return
Gol-lee, Dad burn!
I brought a huge bucket!
I aimed to please!
Get tons of cheese
And tote it back, or truck it!
But blame my wife!
She packed no knife—
I had no way to slice it!
Oh, such bad luck!
I owned no truck,
No way to pack or ice it!
Bam! Man on Moon
Yelled, *You! Baboon!*
Doan monka wid ma cheeses!
So I say, *Hell!*
I might as well
Go home and count my fleases!

POETICITIS

Of things that get you, counting sin,
Diseases still most do you in.
Like tonsilitis, elephantitis,
Shingles or all-out bronchitis,

Pneumonia yet or plain old itch,
Nor count food poisoning, of the which
It takes not much to lay you away
Say from Thursday 'til Monday.

Near least, of course, is appendicitis—
And very worst is this poeticitis!
Which is a herpes of the mind
Two whole shades worse than halt or blind.

You grow restless, four in the morning,
Because rhyme is still a borning;
You toss and turn, you cannot sleep
Until you write it down to keep,
Then turn and toss a wee bit longer
Hoping nothing else goes wronger.

Give me any day appendicitis
In place, dear God, of poeticitis!
Docs take appendicles while you're sleeping,
But poeticitis is for keeping!

SELFISH

Just like Daddy I took my lease
    And claimed my patch of ground;
'Bout the prettiest little piece
    For miles and miles around.
And like Daddy I ploughed my ground
    Faithful and well, knowing
Good harvest one would understand
    If he did the sowing.

With tender care I moved each tree
    To make the small new ground.
And when one day I went to see
    With great delight I found
Back up the branch in moss and trees
    A small but magic spring;
Clearest water one ever sees,
    And pure as everything.

So in the evening, hot and tired,
    I lingered there to drink

Until one day, surprised and mad,
    I looked along the bank
And there were all these strange new tracks
    Stomping about my spring;
I could not figure whose they were,
    But above everything,
I had thought this my very own;
    I wished to share with none;
So I went off, sad and alone,
    Shadowed by evening sun.

One thing for sure; I hadn't seen
    Who'd been there to loiter,
But I remembered Daddy said:
    Son, don't drink the water
Unless you know who owns a spring,
    And who tramps around it.
Pure spring water should belong
    To the man who found it.

So let no man his dipper bring
Thinking to dip another's spring.
And low the thief at night who slips
To someone else's spring and dips!

THE ARTIST'S LAMENT

The Artist creates with his brush,
The Poet with his pen,
But fame and fortune make no rush
'Til after death
        And then
Some Pundit judges up or down
Depending on his mood,
While long we wait for Lady Fate
To bring fine wine and food.

It's late—too late!
        We could not wait!

We've long since departed,
Leaving behind our claim to Fame,
Long dreamed, never started.

*CRADLED IN HELL, DIED IN A THICKET

Hear this sad tale.
                    Old Jiminy Cricket
Went for a hunt, got caught in a thicket,
And since, not a word from Jiminy. . . . So
We'll just have to face it—
                    Let the Old Boy go!

Some good nabor can fetch her wood.
Truth is, Old Jimmy wasn't all that good.
Always fishin' and if weeds took the corn
Well, Jimmy quit worryin' the day he was born.

Real nice feller stopped by t'other day;
Too bad about Jimmy . . .
                              He spent the day,
Found Jimmy's axe, split all the wood;
Did the work better than Jim ever could.
So it's so long, Jimmy, and fare you well—
No man returns from Rhododendron Hell.

* *In the far reaches of the Great Smokies many stories*
Are told about Rhododendron Hells so thick the sun never
Shines through, and a man once disoriented and lost inside
Can never find his way out.

A TALE OF TWO HIKERS

Tipsy Tootle and old Dan Doodle
Set out to hike the Smokies;
Said one to t'other, *I bet we can,*
And I think we will, by hokies.

So they started to roam from Clingman's Dome
Down toward Lake Fontana,
With knapsacks full of taffy pull,
And a long lean green banana.

Soon Tipsy fell in a Rhododendron Hell
Because, Oh, sakes alive, he
Didn't see where the trail had been marked
And he realized suddenly that he was parked
In a bed marked *poison ivy!*
All scratched and bruised, they cruised and cruised
'Till darkness overtook them;
Their feet were fouled where Black Bear prowled,
Their Friendlies all forsook them.
But terror went away when broke the new day
And the Ranger fellows found them.
The strange deep Park is no longer a lark—
Their wives straightway did ground them.

HOUSE-HUNTING ON A SUNDAY AFTERNOON

She jogged along the graveled path
    And nodded a *good day.*
I said *Excuse me, Miss, somehow*
    I must have missed my way.
Turn left, she said, *about a mile,*
    Then right along Pea Ridge,
There you'll find the big white house,
    First one beyond the bridge.
I knew their orchard was for sale
    After last year's freeze.
She paused and frowned and then she said
    They're cutting those oak trees!

Sir, do you plan to live up there?
    Not really, I said, *not really;*
Just like to see big old houses.
    I felt that sounded silly.

Once I looked at James B. Duke's
  Fifty three rooms, I swear;
Met their offer, then they said,
  Historic! You live there!

I drove on to find the house,
  Dreaming, could I live there—
But not if up from river slope
  They had laid the forest bare.
They had!
      I turned back to *Six Mile,*
Nine Times and *Rocky Bottom.*
Place names they were, so picturesque!
  That place has really got'em!

From Walhalla's higher hills
  I gazed back on the lake,
A low-set fog was drifting in,
  A peaceful scene to make.
Two hours more and I was home
  Among familiar faces,
Still dreaming. How nice 'twould be
  If I could live both places!

STRING ON MY FINGER

  At the office:

This to remind me. Home I'll go
And leave it tied here, so I'll know.

  Later, at home:

This bright red string? I'll be jiggered!
That thing worked, just like I figured.

I even know just when and where—
That string has worked like magic, sir.

There's only this small point forgot—
I'm well reminded, but—of what?

MEASURE

Nut brown, copper, bronze or black
    White, yellow, tan—
Color may make the clothes on a rack
    But not the man.

Two carats of a polished gem
    Laid by two rough
Seem worlds apart, to glance at them;
    It's not enough.

For, sandalwood to wide-grain oak,
    Mere paint will hide;
The finish does not make us folk,
    It's what's inside.

READY FOR BED

One day I scrubbed Life's mirrored glass
    Where dimly I could see
Just down the road a falt'ring step.
    My God, I thought, *that's me!*

So if my mind grows quite unclear
    And feet refuse to go,
Cubicle me in no old home
    To fret and drag out so.

I'll feel the twilight of the day
    When it envelops me;
Folk then won't go by what I say,
    Or where I want to be.

Oh, I may be a stubborn child
    Who doesn't want his bed,
But You know best. I'll need the rest;
    Lord, You go right ahead.
                Put me to bed.

OAK RIDGE

Black is the night
forever is winter
home is under the hill.
the hunter is hunted
bold is the eagle
the bear is bolder still.

No more is love
none claims his neighbor
the keeper flees with the key.
sunset is fatal
ski is a poison . . . .
nuclear exit for me.

THE CAST-OFF

Out of you bosom, O Great Mother,
swarm the dread locusts
to devour my life-sustaining leaves;
my bark is stripped, my oneness consumed
in the noisy mouths of them.

I am trapped fatally in the Flower's honeyed sweetness
to drown at last in my own bitter juice.
My soul has been robbed of its barns-full eternity,
even as I stood on the mountain
trying to find my way.
I am bereft of all hope
except I come to You.

Curled fetally, from far beginning,
I await the fall of the knife
which never seems to come.
Time languishes and forever
there is no binding together, no love.

On the night wings of a far-flying Lucifer
I orbit so far that I extinguish totally—
a spent star, never very bright, to plop dully in some Black
    Hole—
I can never escape this exorcism of the Cosmos;
I shall be no more; a nothing that has come to pass.

O Great Mother Universe, I pray waste me not forever
from the all-encompassing circle of your Love.
May two minds on Time's vast ocean come to be as one.

ONE MORE SPRING

The titmouse calls from the juniper tree,
    Robins skip on the lawn;
Another winter has fled; for me
    Spring tip-toes in dawn.

And, oh, how fast the days and years
    Press lately, trooping by;
As sure as laughter has it tears,
    I fear them, nor know why.

Perhaps for me that lonesome call
    From high up in the tree;
Maybe summer will bring no fall,
    But only the end of me.

ENOUGH

I am done with Lost Causes,
Crushed Petunias and Crocodile Tears.
Gluttons!
They feed upon themselves,
Only to vaunt in public their wasted bleeding hearts.

I am done with those who loudly proclaim
That I am born only to faucet myself dry
So they may suck from me my very soul
And claim it as their own.

Helping hands are God-sent,
Extended without constraint to those who truly need.
I would extend mine with humility,
Thankful that so far I have been spared.

But for those who would lay upon me
The guilt for great grandfather
Already six times removed;
Those who would fault me to ten times ten
For what I did not do;
Those who really want no succor
Except to feed on fresh-spilled blood in joyful revenge;
Those who hate would pull me down
To drown with them in their self-induced misery,
From this day forward I will have nothing to do.
I would whack them back
With bush axe and dull machete,
Leaving this time only a bloody stump!

NOT ALONE

Faint steps far back I thought I heard.
    I said *They are my own.*
There's nothing here but Mother Earth.
    I walk this path alone.

Only an echo? The sound grows
    To fill my canyoned walls;
Am I the only one who knows
    That someone out there calls?

NIGHT MOOD

The softness of that summer night
    Not long before we end it;
Our jingling pockets full of youth
    And no care where to spend it.

A medley now of summer sounds
    Drifts in from the stillness;
Our new-found world is out of bounds
    With dreams that leave us will-less.

BACK DOWN ON THE FARM

I caught crawdads in our spring branch
    Where now a rippling lake;
I swam in old Andersen creek,
    Wandered its dark cane brake.

I tracked a mule down furrows
    Stretched out it seemed miles long;
Hoed the corn and milked the cows,
    Heard the whip-o-will song.

I ate ice cream Saturdays
    If Father brought the ice;
Noticed Amy turn sixteen;
    Thought her figure nice.

Corn shuckings marked long Fall nights,
    And frost helped strip the cane;
I nursed my blisters from hard work,
    But heard no one complain.

OLD CHIMNEY, AFTER THE FIRE

I saw an old chimney
Stand gaunt and lone
After the fire.
How lonesome it looked,
How thoughtful:
Like some troubled spirit
Whose grave has been stirred
By meddlesome, curious hands.

This old chimney
Standing alone in the night
Was thinking.
It was not alone.
There were memories—
Memories of the fireside,
Of a snowy wint'ry eve,
   A birth,
         A wedding,
             A death—

Memories to make it smile,
And memories, ah,
Bitters its regret.
The wind stirred
Down the old chimney;
I heard it calling me
Even as I went away
Not to leave it there
Alone in the night.

But faster I ran,
Faster and farther away
From this gaunt old chimney
In the chill of that Autumn night.

It reminded me of a man
Who has trafficked and bartered his soul;

Now
He is left with his memories;
Alone,
With no soul.

CONFLICT

My Soul is a dreamer
  Seeking the heights,
Weaving thin woof
  Of starlit nights.

No longer the valley
  To Soul has worth,
But deep in my being
  I grieve for earth.

My feet seek the meadows,
  My hands, new sweat;
For born of the furrow,
  Heart is there yet.

SONNET TO SHAKESPEARE

Bard of Avon, look kindly back to me,
Nor scornful be of weak and fledgling muse;
For you stood all the world, its golden cruse
Set by the gods and filled with melody.
For you, choicest quill from an angel's wing
And blackest inks from the midnight of hell;
For you, as puppets thrown under your spell,
Came prince or pauper, ghoul or ghost and king.

For me but the fragments—a splintered pen
And these dried dregs of long-forgotten ink
That, scavenged from Time, I remix and use.

Gleaning in vain where genius has been,
I die of thirst by whole flagons of drink;
I sip but gall from my own leaden cruse.

PARTNERSHIP

Summer came, but not the rain;
Our fields were dry as dust;
Not one bit of moisture came
To help earth stir its crust.

Evenings I trudged with water pail
To each bedraggled bed;
Mornings I knew I'd rise to find
My withered stalks all dead.

By and by God stayed the drought,
And like Him once entombed
My flowers raised their heads and lived;
Then, by and by, they bloomed!

In riotous color there I saw
A hundred flashing hues;
By night their fragrance filled the air—
All count I had to lose.

But how my tired heart filled with pride
In each bursting pod;
My one small task had made for me
Partnership with God!

WILD GEESE FLYING

I saw the wild geese flying
    Against an autumn moon.
    All day came their chanted croon,

As on till dusk they whelled by, flying
South and ever to the South
    To some far-off lagoon.

All winter I'll look for wild geese flying
    Against a silver moon;
    And to myself I'll say: Soon,
Soon I'll hear the spring winds sighing,
Soon the wild geese will be crying,
Soon Summer will wing North—flying
With my prodigal Soul, wild geese lying
    Close to a thin new moon.

QUESTION

I think and plan so many things
    I'd sometime like to do;
Then I wonder if I'm queer,
    Or if you're like that too.

LAID BACK

Dragon Fly perched on leafy pad,
Dreaming and riding the eddy.
The quick stream madly rushes by.
Surely that Dragon Boy can fly
When he decides he is ready.
But he loves that placid eddy.
The calm and peace of that pad.
He doesn't see Frog at ready,
Now stalking fat little fly
Sound asleep on his floating pad;
He doesn't see life rushing by;
He thinks not of trouble
Even as you and I.
                    Poor Fly!

THE ERRANT LAWYER

My Lawyer's a procrastinator.
Sooner for his is spelled *later.*
It's not his work, it's those long waits;
I burn while he procrastinates.

Sometimes it's months before he acts.
When he's ready I've lost my facts.
I just want him to hang the guys
For all their lies and alibis.

I implore him—Dang it! Sic'em!
Corral the thugs! Jail'em! Trick'em!
But comes court day and one is dead,
One doesn't show and one has fled.

So smart ol' me, I hold his fee,
Thinking he might turn wiser;
He did me in with one sly grin,
And pulled his big surpriser.

What the heck! I'd mailed his check;
His saw was on my limb!
But came his ace—he'd won the case!
He knows I must have him!

WAY DOWN IN NORTH CAROLINA

There's tar for your heels;
You'll know how it feels
    To raft down the Nantahala.
There's fun everywhere,
You'll dance in the square
    In one big celebration gala.

111

From mountains to sea
You can always be
    As happy as ever you dare—
Old North Carolina,
The state that is finer,
    Will melt your every care.

FOUR POEMS ON FLYING

FLIGHT

I think of wings
Not as the curved anatomy of living things,
    Feathered, pinioned, rounded or sheathed;
    Nor as golden appendages, so long believed
To be the genesis of movement,
    As God conceived.

Wings for me
Match fuselage to nacelle rings;
Wings are slendered, knife-edged, silvered things
    That have no motion of their own
    But the singing of the wild wind, the steady engine
      drone,
    As they slip swiftly through the vortex of Time,
                    carry me on
To Destiny.

THE TAKEOFF

The wing snugs up to the mother sky
    And sounds of earth are stilled;
A wild free wind goes rushing by
    With melody sweet filled.

The lonely hawk backs up nor sees;
    We pass him quickly by,
Lifting up from his sea of trees
    And earth to blazing sky.

Oh, the song of the wing is sweet
    As we move up and on,
For sky and hawk and I shall meet
    Where earth fades and is gone.

NIGHT FLIGHT HOME

Now, to come suddenly upon the town!
My map and my compass point to it there,
But the mountains lie all darkened and bare
Till from the home stretch I can look down
And, spread out before me, there is the town!
The bridge, the river I see, and the trees,
And my heart leaps up, for the sight of these
Is a tonic to me. This is my town!

Then I know. Be the years but one long flight
No heaven can boast a lovelier sight
Than to fly from the dark night and find them,
These clusters of lights, heaven's diadem,
Strung over the hills, running up and down
Like guardian angels over my town.

PILOT'S DREAM

Some perfect day, under a perfect sky,
    I shall walk out to a crowded flight line,
    To a sleek silvered ship that I call mine,
And head straight up; ask any pilot why.

Contrail of a jet will leap into flame
    Against the last rays of the dying sun;
A bright evening star, I forget its name,
    Will be leading the sheep out, one by one.

I shall pause near the end of the runway,
    Twiddling radios, checking the gauges;
I shall think once more: What a lovely day!
    As I warm up the motor, by stages.

Ether will crackle, suddenly alive,
    As all Earthling misgiving I shake off;
Then, my number, "Seven, six, zero, five,"
    Says the tower, "you are cleared for take off!"

I shall deepen my motor's light sweet sound
    With a long firm pressure on the throttle;
Dull earth will fade; we shall leap from the ground
    Like a fly shooting up from a bottle.

WHY I SING

Verse for me is not merely a pastime, even a passion;
it has become a herpes of the mind;
a perennial, spring-erupting disease
embedded long ago in the genes
my mother passed on to me . . . .
I remember her as she sang the old gospel songs,
pumping away at the fancy little mirror-top organ
that always sat in the front room.
Rhythm was in her hands, her dishwashing;
rhythm captivated her soul.
Not surprising that some of it should rub off on me . . . .
but I didn't repeat the pattern.
I tried to create, not echo,
putting together words in little patterns that rhymed.

A lot of folk today don't think much of that.
So a Robert Frost I am not,
but I've seen his very same two roads in the yellow wood,
right here in these Smoky Mountains,
and being my mother's son I wanted to take both of them.

Frost was closer to the land;
a kinship my father insisted on at first, but it was not to be.
I endured the blisters of wood-lotting,
the backaches of long drudging hours in the fields,
but it never came through to me.
Father tried, but Mother was there first.

To please some Critic I shall not now disavow the planting of
     me
that my mother cultivated and encouraged.
I cannot tell myself that a poem is not much of a poem if it
     rhymes.
It goes against my very soul to have all that melody
bubbling as in father's old molasses cooker,
only to be skimmed off and thrown away,
just so some critic may say,
Ah, that's so much better!

And maybe he still would be unmoved;
I'm no Carl Sandburg either.
I've only glimpsed those Chicago fogs
moving on little cat feet
as they slip, slide and slither down the backsides
of my Smoky Mountains, raising not a bit more noise;
and I doubt that Sandburg ever saw
a Smoky Mountain panther.
                              I have.

With the same turning away that I would have liked
on a Saturday afternoon when there was a ballgame down in
     the pasture
but I had to plow, hoe or mend fence,

I now resist much of this prosiac jumble called poetry
they espouse today as the *in* thing.

Like thin shards the words seem tossed in a box.
the trick is to put together,
guess what image the poet projects;
if too clear, too easy, he is shallow;
if vague, maybe, just maybe, he's great!
But how will you know, if the image fails to come through?

Give me the river soft-circling my hill,
  And woods-smoke from the hearth fire;
A moonlit meadow; a night Whip-poor-will
  In pleading tones of desire.
So what if the rhyme beats in stately time
  Or dances lilting tunes?
My mother played hymns, but thought in rag-time;
  She showed me strange new moons.

On the other hand, good poetry doesn't have to rhyme.
Truly great poetry often does not,
yet has everything, including my envy.
Good free verse takes a much better craftsman to do the job,
but so many who are trying today are not good craftsmen.
After all these years I cannot really face up to the challenge,
although I do try occasionally.

Perhaps down that other road in the yellow wood, Mr. Robert
  Frost,
I'll meet up with you some day.
Don't move over yet, Mr. Sandburg;
I don't even own a banjo!
But when pianos get that easy to carry,
I'll sing with you from some far Smoky Mountain.

IMPATIENT MARINERS

Time is the dark sea, shoreless, unknown.
Spawned in its vortex, we are thrown
Outward from depths to limitless space,
Skittering, moving across Time's face,
Splashing, bubbling, sinking to place.

Time is eternal.
                        Time does not pass.
We are the ones who hoist our mass
Of spar and sail to set swift pace
Across unmoving, infinite space.

REAPER MACHINE

Whirring blades,
  Clackety-clack;
Bundles of grain
  Stack,
  Stack;
Endless stubble
Where was wheat;
Man.
Machine.
Dust.
Heat.

Water. A pause.
Drive chain broke.
Monotony.
Noise, smoke.
Then again
It goes, it goes;
Tall wheat wavers,
Stubble grows.

Whirring blades,
Clack,
Clack;
Dirt, sweat,
An aching back.
Blistered hands
Against hot steel,
While turns and turns
The cleated wheel.
An humble vassal
Through heat and dust
Man follows this monster,
Quenches its lust,
Feeds it, bathes its
Stiff joints in oil;
And hand to throttle
Sweats homage to toil.

COBWEB SWEEPERS

I like to walk a city street
    I've never been before
And gaze at all the smart display
    In each big downtown store.

Till finally the shops grow small
    Behind their dingy fronts,
And dust highlights each cobweb spread
    For many, many months.

I like to think, perhaps these men
    Who own each little place
When young would too have asked much more,
    But wisely would not face

The nervous, ulcered way that Life
    Handles cobweb sweepers—
These men instead chose just to be
    Long-lived small storekeepers.

DEATH

Death rides our highways—sudden, swift
    Death walks beside our way;
Death breathes so close we feel his chill
    So many times we say.
And yet this Death, an alien thing,
    Strangely is passed by,
Despised, ignored, denied by we
    Who so soon now must die.

I pray his rendezvous with me
    Be brutal not or stark—
Slapped down some mountain pass alone,
    Hurtling through life's dark;
Nor yet from some atomic split,
    Or boat debris or plane—
May Death at last come up to me
    Like April's cooling rain.

May dimming light of earth remove
    My fevered will to live;
May Heaven reach her arms for me
    And strength and succor give.
Then may I finally know Death
    As staunch and faithful friend,
And through Death know life is the start,
    The grave is not my end.

INDUSTRY MOVES TO THE SMOKIES

My Golden Delicious were just beginning to bloom.
Damn me! Why so civic-minded?
Me and my missionary chamber of commerce work!
For years I had preached, long and loud,
Get industry! Get industry!

Now all at once industry came brawling out of the North,
Fleeing the merciless unions. Up and down my Smoky
    Mountains
Industrialists were taking a look. Their DC 3's, sleek Aero
    Commanders
And Beech Baron C's kept circling, circling overhead.
For I had said, year after year I had said to them:
Here is paradise for all your new plants. This is labor, raw,
    unspoiled;
Mountain men and women, eager, seeking work.
Come, make here your paper and your plastics in these
    abundant waters;
Assemble here your assemblies;
Pour needed dollars into reaching eager hands.

I didn't think once about my apple trees.
Not until the afternoon we borrowed the undertaker's black
    Cadillac,
Met the Big Man's DC 3, and wheeled him royally down my
    half mile
Of graveled road from US 19A to the twenty acres.
Now it was too late!

The man said *It is a good site.* My heart sank,
Even ever so much I wanted the plant. Industry is a must, I
    scolded myself.
It is a community's life blood. *Industry is a must.*
I could stay here forever, I thought I heard him say.
He took a deep breath, looked once more across my twenty
    acres
That lay along the river.
I knew he was breathing apple trees just now pinking bloom.
He was seeing—not big smokestacks, glass, mortar, brick;
rows of parked Chevies and Fords, mountain boys and girls
    hurrying to work—
He was peering into fields of other years before he became the
    Big Industrialist.
A pleasing barefoot memory all his own, with long-gone apple
    trees.

Dear God, how I hated to lose those trees!
I knew in my heart that to pay the Great Society
All that awful tax on something that once upon a time
I had bought for a few sweat-earned cartwheel dollars per acre
Even though new selling for several thousand shrunken
    simoleons per—
I could not take ten times that easy-come money and buy me
    another tract.
Not anymore. Not with TVA, the Forest Service, and even the
    Cherokees
Holding three of every four; not with half of Florida bent on
    buying the rest.

It takes so long, so long, from mountain land
To big full-round Golden Delicious.
I know I shall have no time again, nor suitable land.
Mountain boys and girls will have work and full dinner pails.
Most of them, in their mountain tradition, will plant apple
    trees,
Spotting them along the steep slopes behind their little white
    and red-stained houses
All up and down these wonderful smoky hills.

But the Man seemed to understand about my apple trees.
It is important; someone must understand.
And if I linger not too long upon the branch,
Perhaps I shall miss the few trees and my twenty acres
Much less than I think.

ACAPULCO BAY

Come sunset or daybreak, come middle of the day,
Midnight or midmorning, there's Acapulco Bay.

But it's when the beacon flashes . . . *Clock-wise* . . . *dull* . . .
    bright . . .
And pedlars, guitars and melody haunt the night;

When the cruise ship in the harbour is festive bright with
lights,
And mountains snuggled to blue sky are sleeping through
long nights;

When the daytime emerald aqua darkens fast away,
And the sky is as the water—that's Acapulco Bay!

ACAPULCO IN MAY

The ocean slaves about the feet
    Of Mother Earth and washes
Her white sand beaches nice and neat,
    Or tends her dying marshes.

A wasteland reaches for the sea,
    Though never quite to take it;
An ocean rushes back to me,
    And never quite can make it.

For when I turn all I can see
    Are mountains up and down
Ringing in an emerald sea,
    A sparkling high-rise town.

Soon home on swift-winged jet I go
    Back to my Smoky Mountains;
So long, Gringo, Acapulco;
    And goodbye, Land of Fountains.

GOD COUNTED *THREE!*

And God said to Adam, "This garden plan
Was made just for you. Man, oh, Man!
You have here everything you ought to need—
Garden tools, fertilizer, all kinds of seed—

This spot deep and shady where the flies are few,
And the gnats don't bite but the fishes do.

What you may think is one man's opinion,
But honestly, Adam, your dominion
Is a neat little kingdom; 'bout the sweetest,
Most easily run, most repletest
With all that Man ought to aspire to—
Nothing to bother, aggravate, tire you.

You have running water, even temperature,
Hollow log to sleep in, an' fer sure
No carousin' neighbors stayin' up late
A-swingin' out front on a creaky gate;
No early risers, workin' th' factory,
Borrowin' things, never bringin' back to ye.

Yes, sir, Adam, you sure got it made—
Green crops agrowin', settin' in th' shade,
Sunnin' when you feel like it, lazyin' on,
Your garden is cool, Man.
                                        Gone, real gone!"

Then Adam spoke, "You mean this new plan,
So flexivistuous, just for Man,
Has a key to the Apple House, Lord, thrown in?"
(And here's when the Serpent done gone in!)

"Look, Adam," said the Lord, "there is one thing
    And you ought to keep it straight in your noodle:
Fool around that Apple House, Boy, and you'll bring
    My razor strop on your skadoodle!

"Right back of the Apple House, locked and sealed,
Is a big high fence a-circling a field,
And right in the middle a great bushy tree—
That's an Apple Tree, Boy—
                                        Heaven sent to be

The one thing boys are not meant to touch.
Now look, Adam, is it asking too much
If I just say, 'Go, Boy, where you please;
Fish, swim, climb my sycamore trees;
Gather nuts and plums, feast like a king—
But apples?
                    Son, Apples just ain't the thing.' "

But Adam said, "Well, fud dey O!
I wanted to see the apples grow.
I don't have to pick 'em, or fool with the tree—
I'll be just as good as good can be—
But please, Lord, let me just peek through that fence
And see if they're Winesaps or yellow Quince!"

Then the Lord, knowing well the heart of a boy,
    Said, "Very well, Adam; go look,
While I take a walk here and sort of enjoy
    This scenery down by the brook."
And the Lord left Adam a-headin' toward that fence,
A-hurryin' to see if that tree was a Quince!

When the Lord got back from his scenery,
First off He glanced toward His Apple Tree.
There, under His fence, near the size of a gremlin,
Was a ragged hole.
                        Apple leaves a-tremblin'
Led the Lord's gaze right on out to the top;
And then the Lord thundered,
                                "Adam!
                                    Stop!
That's the one thing, Boy, I did not include!"—
And down
            fell
        Adam.
                    He was scratched and nude!

Oh, some as still think Boys just will have fun,
But the Lord shook his head as He counted to *One.*

124

Now the Lord looked down on recalcitrant Man
   Till He finally settled on Noah;
Said the Lord, "Look, Lad, trip not on your beard,
   But I want you to hurry.
             Go-a
Long to the boat works, draw you a plan;
You'll soon need a boat.
                Hurry, Man!
"There's no time now to be explainin'—
Weather Man says it's to start rainin',
And on and on for forty days
It will rain.
         That's gonna raise
These creeks and bayous. This is no dud—
Noah, Lad, prepare for a flood!"

Now Noah was smart, and he understood—
First he and his sons cut gopherwood,
A monstrous, mountainous stack;
Then off they went for barrels of pitch, stiff and thick and
      black.

From the gopherwood Noah stripped all the bark—
No slum houser, Noah, he was buildin' his ark—
No federal housing, no bankers, no loan,
No government inspectors had to be shown;
Still Noah was all-fired careful of his wood:
That ark had to float.
               Man, it had to be good!
And so Noah laid her out, high and dry,
While an awful lot of folk kept droppin' by,
Laughing and pointing and mislayin' Noah's tools—
And a Gallup Poll called the Noah boys fools!

Three hundred cubits! Three stories high!
Fifty cubits wide!
          Settin' high and dry!

But in good time the ark was all ready,
Pitched and finished, stable and steady.
The animals, as specified, went aboard;
All provisions safely were stored—
Everything seaworthy right to the letter;
In fact, this time, Noah went the Lord better.

But God, knowing well what never would mix,
Soon after caught Noah in a right smart fix.

"Lord, I wasn't," pled Noah, "just being hell-bented;
I took those figs to eat; they must've fermented.
And of course when I happened to taste 'em,
I just knew, Lord, that we shouldn't waste 'em.

"It must be this rain we've been having, you know,
With the humidity being way up so.
Still, Lord, I'll admit, now that you've asked it,
Instead of that keg, those figs should've been stored in a
    basket!"

Said the Lord, "Noah, I'll never know
Why in this world you treat me so.
First, pretending it's food for the pigs,
You sneak aboard this barrel of figs.
Then you let them ferment and lap up the juice.
Oh, Noah, Noah, what's the use!

"For old time's sake I'll still spare you—"
But, ve-ry slowly, God counted to *Two!*

III

He was treed, you could tell. This was Destiny's Hound.
And the Lord said, "Gabriel, what is that sound?"

Then Gabe said, "Lord, Earth's at it again!
Right this minute there are seven men

From Cape Canaveral headed this way,
Rocketing along your fresh-scrubbed way."

And the Lord said, "Gabe, I've told them twice;
It's about time Earth took my advice.
Hot rodding! Missiling! Poisoning Space
With all those atoms.
                                    Man's a disgrace!

"First, Adam broke his word to me
Cavorting up that forbidden tree.
Then just as Noah was proving some use
He snuck on the ark with fermented juice.
Now, look! Our main gate soiled and sagging
From Earth Man's foolish rocket-dragging!

"For this I shall grant no Eternity.
Man keeps goin, he'll reckon with Me!"

But even as the Lord listened afar,
He saw them blast off, felt Earth jar
As Man's huge rockets missiled through Space.
And sadly the Lord turned aside His face.

"Hand me a thunderbolt," God finally said,
"With a point of flame, sharp and red."

Now Man felt the jolt, for Man was upended—
And a great Voice said, "Man, you're suspended—
In an atomized pod that has no doors,
In heaven's elevator, stuck between floors;
Like a mouse in a cheese trap, snozzled to Space,
Watching a clock that has lost its face;
Stuck to a vacuum, wedged in a crack—
No heaven ahead, no gravity back."

And the Lord pulled the shades in Eternity,
Blew out His stars and counted *Three!*

OUTA PIE, AND SLIM KNEW WHY

The cabin roof leaked.

Quite a bit,

But only when it rained.
Old Lady then would throw a fit
Because one time it stained
Her cherished, prized show-off quilts
She'd toiled for years to make.
And once a sneak leak turned to mold
Dried apples meant to bake.

(Long time no pie; I never asked why!)

Come summer's long daylight hours
Green lizards crawled the logs,
And one summer's long wet spell
Spawned yet more pollywogs.

I wanted bad to fix her roof,
But couldn't roof it wet;
And during all those long dry spells
High up I'd get real dizzy yet.

So I'd have to stretch out on the porch,
Or set.

(I sure could climb no roof!)

Come Fall not one shingle split,
So none was ready dried;
And I was still a-porchin'
To ease my sickly hide. . . .
Sometimes I'd smoke my pipe an' dream
Where th' fish were bitin' good,

But bein' too sick to walk to the crick,
Heaven knows, I never split no wood!

First Fall and then come winter
And I hunkered clost to th' fire.
Ol' Woman had split a little kindlin'
And that had rekindled her ire.
Much hotter, Man, yuh better believe,
Than thet ol' woodstove fire!
Then I knew well jus' sure as hell
That roof I was gonna fix!

Big Jim, my Nabor down th' road
Had his shed all packed with shingles,
Now Jim's no fool, but my best mule
And lotsa pies might sway him.
Then if he begged me to help with my roof,
Well, now I might jus' let him!

Fried pies an' all, by early Fall
Ol' Woman could have a new roof,
Maybe even a right good floor.
That could make her so much pleased
She mightn't be so sore.

As a man ol' Jim's kind-hearted,
Sometimes he acts jus' swell;
                              An' I'm thinkin'
With maybe a few coins clinkin'
He would humor a nabor's sick spell.
(Could be a sure-fire sell!)

So jus' watch when I get well
An' days are long an' sunny;
Life once more could be jus' swell—
An' I'll be workin, Honey!

COUNT ON IT, BUBBA!

Oh, yes! Peanuts roll up a wall
If you push with your nose,
But if just then some blonde walks by
Often the peanut goes!
The thing most needed to do this
Is good concentration.
Some blokes have it and some do not;
Just beats all tarnation
That those who have it give scant thought
When counting successes,
While those who don't just cannot wait
To excuse their messes.

One Bubba counted himself smart;
He sniff-sniffed lots of glue,
But only shells clung to his nose—
The peanuts fell right through.
So don't write off natural law
When well you know it's true;
Your next big fear might well be, Sir,
A greased nightstick or two.

And one thing more, Old Bubba;
                              Man,
Get wise to stunts you do;
All day you can roll peanuts up,
But what good do you do?
You will destroy its racy curve
Playing games with your nose;
Go out and find some worthwhile work
And do it well!
                    Who knows?
You might achieve a lot more fame
If Life were wisely used.
Go choose a better-sounding name
And be no more excused.

Down road could see a monument
Of you right on town square!
But, Bub, we'll need to see results
Before we put it there!

CAUTION

A touch of Bubba
Is in us all;
He must be starved
To keep him small;
Unwatched he could
Stretch ten feet tall!
And that translates
To grief for all!
The lazy Lout
Might eat us out
And never work at all!

NANTAHALA NONSENSE

The Ive and the Ip met a Butter Chip
On their way to the Churling Roil.
Snarled the Butter Chip, "I bet I can whip
You quicker than water can boil!"
"Oh, you can, can you," snarled a Willy Woo
who happened passing by,
"Well, we'll soon see; first you must whip me,"
And he spoke it plain as pie.

The Willy Woo struck a lick or two
And bloodied Chippy's nose.
Cried the Chip, "Boo hoo, I don't like you!
Take that! And these! And those!"

"We can't rent the raft, if we all act daft,
Do as Crazy Lazy sez,
Or we'll lose our oars in the Bogie Roars,
And dump our carcuses!"

"That's right," said the Ip. "so button your lip,
And do as Crazy sez!"

Then linking arms they exchanged charms
And all apologized.
"Sorry, Butter Cup and Johnny O'Up,
We never realized
That we've just trappled your bonnie dappled
Beautiful little blooms;
We've done you wrong, so we'll move along
Out of your living rooms."

So the Ive and the Ip did a double flip
In joyful celebration;
And the Will O'Woo snarled a once or two,
Then puffed up with elation.

And on they went to rent the raft,
Really a great and wonderful craft,
All yellow and piled with wonder;
They paddled gaily down the Nantahaily
In the raft they'd named *Thunder.*

They sailed through the Roil where the Mad Waters boil
And never once went under;
They paddled together through wet and weather,
Never again to blunder.

BIRTHDAY

Today! Long last, this is the day—
We've marked it on the wall.

Look, each mark shows a passing year,
  How much you weighed, how tall.

Today, my son, at last you're six,
  Grown up and oh, so wise;
I see it written on your face,
  In eager, laughing eyes.

I watch the manly things you do,
  The things you think and say;
And how I thrill to be with you
  On this your sixth birthday.

Ah, magic moment, you withdraw
  My worries as a man—
I all but feel the wonder of
  A full-fledged boy again.

But Time is fickle and I know
  The road that I must tread;
For me it stands at halfway mark,
  And for you, all ahead.

So Godspeed to you, Jamie Lee.
  You cannot know how glad
I am that you are six today
  And I can be your dad.

ONE FOR BETH

Write one to me, my child had said;
  Please, Daddy, one for me;
My sister has her poem and
  You must do one for me.

When I looked back my small one had
    A grown-up big-girl look;
College called just down the way,
    But still there was no book.

Soon now, dear one, I've promised you . . . .
    But Time did not hold still;
Just now the daughter of my Beth
    Plays near me. So does Will.

So here's to Beth, my mountain girl,
    Who is today as sweet
As when she tousled on the floor
    To nestle near my feet.

Sorry the poem came so late
    That you felt left apart;
You who so slowly are in book,
    So early took my heart.

MY BLUE-EYED BOYS

I want the very best in life
    To wrap and hand to you;
In fact, there isn't anything
    I guess I would not do

If in the doing happiness
    And all abundant joys
Were given you to dwell with you,
    My sons, my blue-eyed boys.

I want to smooth the rugged road
    Of life that you must tread,
And free you from the stabbing pain,
    The heartache and the dread.

Yet well I know that I cannot
    Live all of life for you;
There are so many, many things
    Each for himself must do.

So Godspeed to you as you go
    Life's sharp, uncertain way;
From dimming shadows I shall watch,
    And hope, and trust, and pray.

PLAN FOR ANN

I like to take my baby girl
    And toss her in the air,
Or tease and tickle her until
    I've mussed her dress and hair.

I ask to see how far she can
    Stick out her tongue at me,
Then have her turn from side to side
    For all the room to see.

I trot her up and down until
    I'm worn out, or the wife
Happens along, and then I'm through
    For you can bet your life

At my house we do not intend
    To bring up any child
As sweet as our own Ann Marie
    To be that rough and wild.

So quietly we settle down,
    Or so the good wife thinks,
For Ann, just barely eighteen months,
    Looks back to me and winks.

NEXT WINDOW, PLEASE

We live such fast-paced lives today,
We're always on the run;
Hardee's, McDonalds, Wendy's
We take Life on a bun!

THE HUNT

Like one who deep in untracked forest
Takes from highest tree
And bears away to castle cage
Bright-plumaged melody,
So seek I now some rare new song
That, captured, will sing on
To brighten other dreary days
After mine are gone.

Not yet, not yet, perhaps never
Immortality,
But still my Soul on some far reach
Seeks its melody;
And how much poorer even to dust
If selfish it should keep
The smallest part of one small song
Down to fitful sleep.

TABLES TURN

I went to see my friend.
Two dogs answered his door.
They wagged me to come in,
And what had I come for.
Old Tom is out both barked,
So what could they now do?

I said it was old Tom
    I'd come to interview.
They then dropped this tall tale:
    Today's Christmas Day!
Since Master's hanging out,
    Please let us have the say!

Christmas is time to share,
    And we will point the way—
Please write first, We love Tom,
    But most when he's away!
Old Tom's tough! He barks rough,
    Sometimes real late at night;
Had three wives, drinks straight Scotch;
    At times he's not real bright!
Still, today we've saved for;
    We've bought this big juice drink.
Just for Tom! Bottoms up!
    Come, Tom! Come on and drink!

You give us water, Tom,
    While you have Scotch, no fail—
This time, Sir, we drink Scotch,
    You'll drink this fruity ale!

NIGHT CRISIS*

This Fly Boy Heel
In his Oldsmobile
    Drove straight at the Blackhawk 'copter.
The Blackhawk had stopped,
But straight up it hopped
    Or the Oldsmobile would stopped her.

So lose all hope
Of carrying dope
    By night in your sleek helicopter.

This Nut at the wheel
Of his Oldsmobile
　　With a bit of luck will have clopped her.

He will break the rotor
On your pop-pop motor
　　His lights out, running wide open;
He will ring the bell
On your door to Hell—
　　And I think that's what he's still hopin'.

A military Blackhawk, about 11 at night, started visiting the Poet's private landing field three nights a week, landing at the far end of the field and staying only about 3 or 4 minutes. It would take off about the time someone could get to the field. We concluded it must be delivering dope. One night on impulse I cut my lights off, floor-boarded the throttle, and headed right toward it. The copter was idling and jumped straight up when I was about 200 feet away. It never returned.

*I AM NOT AFRAID

Old Devil said *Hell!*

　　　　　　This road leads to Hell!
　　Jamie said,

　　　　　　I am not afraid!
Sly Devil waxed stout, tossed Jamie about.
　　Jamie held tight.

　　　　　　He prayed.

Late sun turned red over Jamie's head,
　　His world swirled fast away;
A soul's ebb-tide, a Life's divide,—
　　One question,

　　　　　　Go or stay.

No evening sun, day now was done,
　　Jamie faced darkness, dismayed,
But God reached his hand,
　　　　　Sheep grazed on his land—

Jamie smiled,
　　　　I am not afraid!

---

* *James Lee Sossamon, second son, aero-space engineer, sheep-herder, keeper of the land, fought colon cancer five years, endured a colostmy, tended his sheep, built his log home, did full service in his church, and kept an abiding faith.*

His grave tops a green hillside by the little church he loved, almost in sight of the gentle hills where he tended his sheep. His tombstone mirrors and quotes from his life: I am not afraid!

SORGHUM FALL

Molasses-making time
Stands in my memory still;
The shady trees by the river's bank
And the mule-drawn sorghum mill.

Frosty mornings when we hand-stripped the cane;
The cutting, the stacking, the haul
To a wood-fired oven under the trees
In sorghum time, come fall.

At last the slow-fired, bubbling sirup,
With its golden skimming for beer.
Oh, molasses time, come fall time,
The happiest time of the year!

ANSWER

Lad in the puddle, mud-spattered and wet,
With morning-clean britches so tightly rolled,
How well you should know your mother will scold
Though now you show not the slightest regret.
Muddy hands on hips, chubby legs wide-spaced,
You've such a confident look in your eye—
I know what you mean, those buttresses high,
Holding the last big spanner you have placed.

Yours a new world and you must engineer
(With a pardon for all small, muddy feet);
For the challenge is here; new things to do;
And you the stout-hearted with freckled ear
Will step to the breech nor bow to defeat,
For the future of the world is in you.

THE BOY AND THE OLD THREAD WINDER

He came last night across our marsh. He climbed our little
    hill
And found our path through the poplars tall down by
    Barrier's mill.
He stopped a moment by the bees Grandfather always kept,
Then moved along the flagstone walk like Grandpa used to
    step.

I could not see him but I knew. It hung there in the air.
A sad and heavy sort of thing. I felt it everywhere.

Grandfather turned his head to me and tried to speak once
    more.
But then I heard *him* on the stoop. I saw *him* at the door.

It was an easy, peaceful scene. Grandfather's gentle sigh
Was all that told me I had paid to him my last goodbye.

Then I was glad. I felt somehow I knew about this thing,
For I could see Grandfather's life just as a ball of string

That for these three and eighty years he slowly had
    unwound.
Now there had come a tally score; both tattered ends were
    bound.
No more I doubted. Now I knew.
                    Each little bit of string
Must wind untangled back to God, our final Everything.

ON FORM

Sonnet of softest melody
    Held lightly in my hand,
Made for me, but meant for me
    To love, not understand.

Melodied jewel—pointed, turned,
    And softly calling me—
What Perfection wrote thy form,
    A perfect symphony?

I'VE BEEN HERE BEFORE!

I trod an unfamiliar height today;
    Yet for an instant fleeter than light,
    Like the blinding flash of the meteorite
Burning through space, I seemed to know my way.
Too fast for thought the haunting brilliance fled,
    Till fogs of earth closed fast upon my mind;
    No trace of the passing more could I find—
The far-fetched start, or where it might have led.

But in its glow my Spirit seemed at home
   As soft the brightness lit this barren sod;
I stood to highest heaven, touched her shining dome,
   And walked where only seraphim have trod:
Clay for an instant had let Soul roam—
And, backside of heaven, God had been home.

A SINNER'S PRAYER

Out from Thy vastness, world on world,
   Out of infinity,
Stretch forth a hand, O gracious God—
   Reach it down to me.

Down through the depths of a wasteland world,
   As you search, please, God, see
That humbly I look up asking Thy love;
   Oh, grant it, God, to me!

FACE TO FACE

How high the mountains, O my Soul!
   How winding is my road!
Beyond which summit lies the goal?
   For how long yet the goad?

To toil and climb, to sweat and grieve
   For something vague, unseen—
What yearns within me that I leave
   This valley's pleasant green?

I cannot prove where or when
   Or even *if* Death gives
Somewhere a passage through which men
   Shall meet God where He lives.

But this I know, as mountains bleak
　　Allow these stone-bruised feet,
Glory surrounds some distant peak—
　　There, one day, we shall meet.

PINHEADS AND POLITICIANS

I was scared as hell when I left B.C.
Dodgin' and a-runnin' toward Tennessee.

Where once the Cherokee had stalked
Fleet-footed Black Bear,
　　　　　　　　　Now I walked
With both eyes pelled!
　　　　　　　　　But not for bear!
My foe might still be lurking there.

Sure enough! Right On the old Tennessee line
I saw those arrows a-comin' a-flyin',
Light feather-rigged!
　　　　　　　　　The twang of the bow
Was all the warning I would know.
These were aimed at my gut.
　　　　　　　　　Oh, No!

I'd run so fast I'd already passed
The stake-out where they took their aim;
That gave hope for a new ball game!
Those arrows once aimed at my gut
Were now dead on straight for my butt!

For the record, such wounds, you see,
Get no mention now of bravery.
So I'm real careful when going through Swain
Those pin-headed Pols might try it again.

You see, all Heroes get shot in the gut,
And only cowards get shot in the butt!

Light reference to long-standing
feud between Poet and Politician
In Swain County.

PAST GLORY

When the winds walk tall on the mountain top,
    I'm a coward. I hide me.
While the fir and the spruce crackle and pop
    In their struggle to be free.

They call to the Brave, *Come climb our steep slope.*
    Stop this mad charge of the wind!
They beg for our help, while they cling to hope,
    As Angels who've never sinned.

Go lend a hand, you Heroes all;
    You Brave who must achieve;
But once to the end you cannot extend:
    Past glory you cannot retrieve.

THE TATTERED BASKET

This worn old basket once held plans
    And dreams of younger years;
It now belongs to a bent old man
    Who picks up cans for beers.

His basket filled he trudges off
    Once more his fears to stay
Until the good night wraps him up
    To close his lonely day.

It gives me thought—I'll go look through
    Old dreams that once walked tall;

Sort out old closets, basement trash,
　　Clean up this cluttered hall.

But will I ever? Maybe not.
　　I'm now the stooped old man
Who's grown content with pauper's lot,
　　And lives as best he can.

I can't recall all those young dreams
　　I've lost along Life's road;
I limp along, but sing no song;
　　I'm burdened with my load.

THE CHOICE

Oh, to kneel at the pit
To feel the wind and fire

　　　　　　　　　　　　　　to know

To peek in
To ask God how

　　　　　　　　　　and when.

Some say thousands of years ago it began
Other Wise Men, scientists,
Say billions of years.
They tell us that
In the Big Bang
With its magic mists
Floating remnants
That first burst of creation
Came rock, great rivers of flame,
Mountains, our earth.

So where is Truth?
With me with God there is everything, or nothing.
With the rest, nothing.

SMART BUGGER

How knew that Ant the sugar spilled?
　　It made no noise in fall.
But he rushed in and dined.
　　　　　　　　　When filled,
　　Cell-phoned his cousins;
　　　　　　　　　All
Quickly formed one long straight line,
　　Marched soldier-like,
　　　　　　　　　And, look—
Had they been elephants I know
Our whole house would've shook!

Now you tell me how that Ant knew
　　About the spilled sugar?
I surely have no clue,
　　　　　　　　　Maybe,
　　Young Ant one smart Bugger!

MY BIG REQUEST

God gave us relatives,
Then said, "You'll need some friends."
In his left-handed way
He meant to make amends.
Close of kin may sue you,
But true friends seldom will;
If your kin wreck your car,
You'll get the repair bill.

Win the big lottery,
Kinfolk termite your floor,
Each toting a large sack,
And tunneling for more.

Invite them to dinner,
They eat and eat a lot;
Then take your roast with them
And don't return the pot.

One smart one claimed bad luck
Until I signed his note.
He skipped. Left me to pay.
He beat me, danged ol' Goat.

Fall deep down in a ditch,
Hurt, helpless, near to die;
And not one kin shows up to help,
Or muddy your good eye.

So just use simple math to
Divide and multiply;
Relatives turn rabbits;
Friends crawl off to die.

So, Lord, next time you wish
To offer more amends,
Go easy on the kinfolk—
Just send me lots of friends!

FIREFLY

The firefly is some bug, but still
    He rates my sympathy
Because in bugdom I am sure
    No use for him can be
Except to flit, the silly thing,
    Until he blows his fuse
With flashing on and flashing off
    Till no sane bug can use

The sparks from off his dynamo
　　For even simple power.
This goofy bug just wastes away
　　His wattage by the hour.

How vastly more successful would
　　The firefly find the night
If he would just calm down and give
　　His world a steady light;
And also if he could remake
　　His queer anatomy
And bring his tail-light to the front
　　For visibility.

FIREPLACE

A fireplace is a pleasant place
　　I think without a doubt,
And something that each home should have
　　To gather friends about.

The man-made fire it holds will keep
　　Wintery chills at bay
And lend a brightness to a room
　　That chases gloom away.

Memories seasoned on its hearth
　　Outlive the skeptic's scorn,
So heap more yams in ashes deep
　　And bring some popping corn.

For even though the basement holds
　　A big old furnace that
Sends heat by pipe to every room
　　At bid of thermostat,

I still delight to sit and talk
 Before my open grate
Until the embers die away
 And night is growing late.

THINGS I LOVE

A country lane in lilac time
 Where bees seek sweet perfume;
A thicket near a forest filled
 With honeysuckle bloom.

The first soft drifting of the snow
 At night in early fall;
Our search for fern and mistletoe
 To deck the banquet hall.

An open fire of great green logs
 While fierce winds howl and blow,
Popping and cracking as they did
 In forests long ago.

The first faint stirring of the spring
 Across earth's frozen breast,
Pulsing with life a whole new world
 After the winter's rest.

Starlight and moonmist far to East,
 With summer's sky above—
These are a few of many things
 In life that I most love.

TRIP TO TOWN

Big cities are seductive when
 I feel their urge, and so

For three or four tall frenzied nights
   I scurry to and fro
From club to hall to cinema,
   From stadium to ring,
Madly spending energy
   And money in the fling.

But quickly tiring of it all
   I turn my aching feet
To seek once more the peace of home
   Along my village street
Where lights burn low by evening and
   The noise is far away;
Where slumber takes me trailing dreams
   Till bright eyes greet the day.

PROGRESSION

To live is to hope,
To hope is to pray
That each tomorrow
Along my way
Be nobler, sweeter
Than yesterday.

OH, DOCTOR!

I never fail to wonder, when
   For doctor I disrobe
And stand for him to pry and push
   And gouge and feel and probe

Until his educated touch
    And my ah, oh, and ouch
Have analyzed the hidden ache
    And driven off my grouch.

I'm more amazed to realize
    Each time I stop to think
That when to doc I hurry so,
    Though poised right on the brink

Of death itself, he jokes and laughs
    Until I force a smile;
So even if my pain remains,
    In just a little while

I feel much better—So to die
    I think I never could,
Unless without doc sometime I
    Just sat and thought I would.

CLEVERNESS

I see so many clever things
    In all the stores I go,
And often I think to myself
    How simple! Why I know

Enough to build a thing like that—
    Most anybody could;
It's just a bolt, a piece of wire,
    A spring, a block of wood.

It took no Edison to think
    And draft its master plan;
The guy who made that thing was just
    Like me, an average man.

Yet while he made a million bucks,
   And will perhaps make more,
On something I knew just as well,
   I really can't be sore

Because the world writes no big check
   To those who say "I knew it!"
They only pay the jackpot to
   The fellow who can do it.

APPLE GROWER

I love the sound a shower makes
   Down through my mountain trees,
Followed by the damp caress
   Of some small playful breeze,
I like to feel beneath my feet
   The firmness of my land,
Soon to produce the summer fruit
   I pluck with eager hand.

I love to see the barren earth
   Conjure grassy cover
And wrap itself in tenderness
   As lover clasped to lover.
Such little things I love so, and
   How awful it will be
If heaven has no such in store
   For pilgrims who like me

Do not enjoy the footsore crowd
   That hurries up and down
To seek its wealth in public place
   From town to dusty town,
But who, as I, prefer to dwell
   In quietness and peace
Beneath our apple trees until
   God calls us from our lease.

FORTY WINKS

I love to climb a mountain slope
　　Until I reach the peak
And sprawl at length there in the grass,
　　Too out of breath to speak.

I like to look far, far below
　　And see the winding way
My path has led me up the steep
　　That I have climbed that day.

But oh! how I detest to go
　　To bed at night and see
Each detailed worry of my day
　　Parade in front of me.

Small help then all the sheep I count,
　　Or effort I exert;
My eyes grow wider by the hour,
　　My brain gets more alert.

And how I envy those who can
　　Smooth out life's many kinks
Just closing shop as turtles do
　　To catch their forty winks.

TODAY

Today is now; we cannot hold
　　Against the press of years,
Or use as closet space to fold
　　Away our many fears.

Today is framed in bits of song
    And ribboned with some sorrow;
Today is a shell in the ocean of time,
    Emptied, beached tomorrow.

Today is a laugh, some lover's tear,
    Dim hope newly begotten;
Today is now: perpetually here,
    Eternally forgotten.

SEEN FROM THE BRIDGE

Another new year with gleaming white pages,
    And Father Time with his ball-point pen,
Our antics make him nervous sometimes,
    Or maybe it's just some men
Who delight as children to smudge his ink
    And hope he doesn't look
As page by page he writes it down
    In his big black book.

So here's to Time! May he give
    To use in fullest measure,
And gently deal with all who smudge
    The ink in his big ledger.

SNOW

I love the crunchy sound of snow
    Beneath a bright new sled,
With swirling drifts along a hedge
    And snow clouds overhead.

I like to see the straggling tracks
    Laid down by boyish feet,

154

Crisscrossing through the fluffy snow
    Along my village street.

I like to press the light white flakes
    Into a firm snow ball
And toss it at some passerby
    To hear his startled call.

But you can blame it on my years,
    I'm just plain getting old,
Or kinder be and simply say
    He cannot stand the cold—

For at the most, one day of snow
    And then I'm sure to say
The snow was nice, but how I wish
    The slush would go away.

SPRING CAMPAIGN

Every spring the wife will get
    An urge to go and dig
Across the lawn some hundred holes,
    And in each plant a twig

Of shrub or flow'r, some root or seed
    She says will soon sprout and
With all the bounty nature boasts
    Make beautiful our land.

But come next day, D-day plus one,
    It also seems quite clear
The thought has reached our neighbor's hens,
    For you have no idea

How quickly all those fowl acquire
    Enough inventive sense

To go and find a low place and
  Dig down beneath our fence.

From then till fall I watch the fray
  As each intently labors;
I quite agree with Robert Frost,
  "Good fences make good neighbors."

TO MY DENTIST

My mother taught me I should come
  To see you twice a year;
That you were kind and gentle and
  I would have naught to fear
And so from childhood I've read all
  Your tattered magazines,
And peered through your old stereoscope
  At those same dog-earred scenes.

I've memorized your wallpaper,
  And know in each small part
Those queer diplomas you have lined
  Across the wall; my heart
Still thumps within my dry, parched throat—
  Though weak-kneed still I grin—
Each time your nurse gets down to me
  With "Won't you please come in?"

I know I'll live, but still I sit
  And squirm there in your chair,
Knowing full well you'll never break
  My neck; you wouldn't dare!
But then it comes, "This won't hurt much,"
  You say with poised pliers—
Oh, why should your kind all turn out
  To be such awful liars!

GRANDMOTHER'S PROBLEM

Oh, goodness gracious goodness me!
What can I buy for a lady three?

Were she ten, domestic and grim,
Busy with her pies, tongue stuck out at Jim,
Betty sick abed and Anna crying,
Tony with the mumps and maybe dying—
I'm sure as sure what it would be:
A ma-ma doll for her family.

Were she sixteen, all ribbons and bows,
With curlpapers twisted in neat little rows,
And a knowing twinkle in her deep blue eyes,
As a birthday giver I should be wise
To send her perhaps a beauty kit
With lipstick and rouge and powder in it;
And in a far corner, in case there was room,
I'd tuck in a dash of dainty perfume,
All fragrant of places by far-off sea
Where her own Prince Charming is sure to be.

Were she twenty, with plenty of beaux,
I'd send a fine gown, but goodness knows
A lady named Shirley, just barely three,
The sense of this would hardly see.
So since she's neither ten nor twenty,
But just three, and grown up plenty,
I'll send her a—ah, you've already guessed?
Well, hardly the use to tell you the rest—
I'll send her a pair of shoes, all red,
To park at the foot of her trundle bed;
To scuff down the stairs and through the hall,
And patter to the room at mother's call;
To keep in her trunk when at my age she
Is buying red shoes for someone three.

LITTLE THINGS

The little things of life I know
So often don't amount
To very much in busy lives
Where only big things count.

Some strive to own a bigger house
Than neighbors down the street;
Others drive a finer car
Than anyone they meet.

And so in order to assure
What only wealth can bring,
We sell our lives to toil and sweat
And forget everything.

That doesn't have a dollar mark
Across the front of it,
Until at last—old, worn and bent—
We top life's heap and sit

With nothing much to do except
Look back along the way
And yearn for all those little things
That once we threw away.

SALESMANSHIP

I find it easy to say No
To smart young salesmen who
Depend less on the thing they sell
Than on their follow-through.
They ooze with personality
That dares me to resist;

The pleasure then becomes all mine
    To check me off their list.

My weakness is some selling fool
    Who comes in awkward guise,
And all is done before I guess
    That he, not I, was wise.
His first approach is timid, and
    I start out telling him
Till inch by inch I've let me crawl
    Too far out on his limb!

I tell myself he hasn't made
    A sale perhaps all week;
That all the business must go
    To chaps who're smart and sleek.
So often when I really don't
    Intend at first to buy,
I talk myself into the thing—
    Then later wonder why.

BANKER

My banker is a friendly guy—
    I rather like the cuss;
He sports a bald spot on his top
    Just like the rest of us.
And though he's punctual for deals
    Much more than you or I,
He has another fellow who
    Is always standing by
To tell him just who, when or what,
    And so keep life in order,
While most of us must get along
    Just hit or miss, sorta.

And then my banker, bless his heart,
    Can never fume nor fuss,
While day by day he sits there and
    Puts up with all of us.
He shares our tale of woe, he knows
    How nearly we go broke—
He must get fed up sometimes till
    He nearly has to choke.
So as for banking, though short hours
    With lots of time to fish,
I'd just as soon be counted out;
    I'll make some other wish.

SEED CATALOG

I think I'll write my congressman
    And earnestly implore
That though we have one million laws,
    I'd like, please, just one more.

The men who write seed catalogs
    My law would force to try
Hard labor growing all the things
    They paint to catch my eye.

Because in not one catalog
    Is ever there a hint
That weeds are faster than the hoe,
    And bugs are not God-meant.

In ignorance they let me gaze
    At pumpkin-sized cherries,
And luscious beans on giant stalk,
    And mammoth boysenberries.

But comes the time to go and pick
    Such wonders from my vine,
Then I'm convinced those catalogs
    Have handed me a line!

CRAZY MARKET

It seems that every time I get
A thing I really like
Along will come some one and give
The price a hefty hike.
First off it was the bungalow
With mortgage and a leak,
Then some old shotgun I had bought
Before inflation's peak;
And then, worse thing, the family car
Upon the block was laid
Because some guy said I will give
Just twice, sir, what you paid.
So now whenever I acquire
A thing that's to my taste
I feel an urge to be a squirrel
And bury it with haste,
For though I like a profit, this
Has me in confusion,
I feel that value has become
An optical illusion.

THE CHURCH

To those who would label the Christ
Largely non-conformist
Or take his ministry to be
That of mere reformist,

I would point out around the world
Those many marble busts
That name to fame great souls who sought
To free this world from lusts,
But in some park alone and cold
Pigeons for their neighbors
Just statues stand to remind man
Of those great souls' labors;
But then you'll note across the world
Stand great wide-open doors
To calm and succor millions as
They tire with earthly chores
And as I see this world-wide church
I'm sure we've over-priced
The value of a dead reform
Above a living Christ.

DOWN HOME

When sun-starved willows start new life
And jonquils upward peek,
From childhood on I've felt the urge
To head for Ander's creek.
Where once the cooling meadow grass
Caressed me as I ran
Some farmer now has drained the swamp
With scientific plan
For now the meadow is a field,
The sandbars have been dredged;
The swimming hole has disappeared,
The creek banks are de-hedged
For Time will change all things, as now
It thins the grayish hair
Of the carefree, buoyant boy
Who once went swimming there,

But one thing time can never take
Deal with me how it will
And that's the urge, when I'm down home
To swim, at Ander's mill.

CAREFUL

Some folk are careful all their lives
Lest some mishap befall,
They always say what you have planned
Will just not do at all;
They warn you of the hazards of
The modern motor car,
They're careful of their liver lest
It get some sudden jar.
Let just one small shy germ appear
And quick they get the Flit
Then probe and peer about until
They've found and murdered it,
But other people sail through life
Somehow quite unaware
Of many of these worries or
They just don't seem to care,
And when the final score is in
Statistically it's bad
The findings do not often make
Insurance people glad
For he who chased out every germ
And took no risk, is dead! The papers say he died last night,
Asleep, at home, in bed!

BUILDER

The mason deftly takes his trowel
And level in his hand,

From mortar board he scoops his "mud,"
His cement and his sand,
Then one by one he takes his brick
And roughened cinder block
Or thoughtfully he takes his pick
From just plain old field rock
But from his skillful work shapes up
Far more than first would seem
For with this mud and brick he breathes
A soul into my dream.
Except for plan of architect
And scale instead of guess
Appearance of the finished dream
Would still be ugliness;
Except for skill of workmen who
Give body to the plan
The building still would merely be
The idea of some man;
So each contributes his small part
There is no wond'rous trick;
It's sweat and toil, and plan and dream
Laid slowly brick by brick.

WEATHER-WISHERS

In summertime we wish for fall
Or snow and lots of ice,
We dream about a blizzard and
Think that would be quite nice,
But in the winter when we count
The chill bumps on our nose
And rub our brittle, stiffened ears
And flex our frosted toes
Our thoughts turn back to summer when
We sought the welcome shade
Or mopped our brows in August heat
And sipped pink lemonade;

So, knowing us, it's best by far
Our seasons are so planned
That we must take what comes, and not
Each order his own brand.

KEEP BUSY

Some say it isn't worth the try
To sit a-top Life's heap
And on a slippery, spinning globe
Scarcely foothold keep,
But even God chose busy men
And deep within the heart
It's natural to want to be
Of busy things a part.
So though you're never president
Nor Mayor yet, nor nothing
You just stick in there near the top
Or die, still in there scuffling,
For when Life's final count is in
And all is lost or won
God's judgment could be based on just
The things you've tried and done.

OUR CHOICE

Grasshoppers have, I'm very sure,
An infinitesimal brain
And as we of some people say
Of wisdom not a grain
Or they would not spend such long hours
In self-esteemed elation
Imposing on a whole wide world
Their noisy stridulation.
Or if in song they do not lend
To noisy confusions

Quite aimlessly they pass the time
Jumping to conclusions
Then let us try quite hard to be
Wiser than we have been;
Let us not act like insects if
God made us to be men.

POLITICIANS

Politicians have a way
Of kissing babies and
With warmth and deep affection they
Rush up and shake your hand.
The cigars that they pass out may
Be big and black and strong
But none so rank I'm here to say
As information wrong
Which often circulates about
And through the big campaign
As each contender thumps the tub
And strives with might and main
To pull some rabbit from the hat
Which will corral the vote
Or at the least will tie up tight
The other fellow's goat.
To every question they will say
A big resounding yes
Even though fulfillment would
Bring on an awful mess
And if some voter should decide
He wants a slice of moon
Pronto 'tis promised, served with tea
Green cheese and silver spoon.
Now why they make these promises
I'm sure I cannot say
It all seems so ridiculous

When comes election day,
For miracle that always is
In high arithmetic
Whether done with mirrors or
Mirage or Hindu trick
The voters may be scarcer than
Ten thousand dollar notes,
But when they count they always find
A bumper crop of votes.

NOTIONS

Sometimes I have the energy
Of some great dynamo
And then again I mope about
And hardly make a go
Of even simple things the wife
Informs me I must do,
But even so, I'm not too queer.
Most folks are like that who
Rate neither up to quiz kid class
Nor down to average dumb
Who live and work from day to day
And take things as they come.
Freud of course would analyze
And tonics by the score
Blame for all such our liver or
The stomach, but the more
I meditate upon these things
The less I think a potion
Would cure my laziness; I think
Much is in my notion.
If I start thinking I am sick
Sickness I'll likely see
Or if I think that life is swell
Then most of it will be.

SOFTIES

We pipe our houses with steam heat
And spurn an open fire;
We vacuum clean instead of sweep
And times are getting dire
If some fine morning we must walk
Just one short extra block
Down to some factory where we sit
And count, and tie and stack
The product that we never touch
Except to feed the tack,
So I should not be much surprised
To see this grand old race
A million years or so from now
Fall into sad disgrace
And shed its arms and legs and feet
Keeping just eyes and ears
For that is all we'll need to live
As super gadgeteers.

HATS

Some people think a woman's hat
Has no rhyme or reason,
That what some dames sprout forth on top
Borders close to treason.
They tell you that a saucepan makes
And looks more like a hat
Than almost anything the femmes
Can bring forth—that is that
But I have carefully surveyed
The case and so conclude
We've been unfair in making fun,
And with our manners crude,
And so I now confess these hats
Reveal in high degree

The inner woman of the mind
For frill and fantasy;
It's just that we must bear in mind
Her personality,
Then by her hat we judge her brain
And that is that, you see.

DECISION

If with some folks you don't agree
They label you as rude,
They mark you down to bargain price,
They tag your manners crude,
But if to everyone you say
I thoroughly agree
Then shortly you will find yourself
In need of sympathy.
Your thought will not be worth the price
Of one small tinker's dam;
You'll lose respect of all your friends
The neighbors doors will slam
Upon your poor nose should you try
To drop back with the crowd,
Your aching head will bloody be
And, brother, oh, so bowed
Then take you time, wait, try to think
Each situation through;
From all the facts make up your mind
Just what you ought to do.

PAPER, MISTER?

A fellow shoots his wife and so
You read it in the news
Replete with details of the crime
And all the gory clues,

Or someone takes a little drink
And cuts a dizzy caper
No harm done, so the fellow says
But still it's in the paper
Right down below is given what
The sermon was for Sunday
Framed in by all the foolish things
Some layman did on Monday
But all who read the paper think
They alone should edit;
That editors are but to blame
After some sap said it.
So publishers and editors
End up in one sad heap
With epitaphs that leave no doubt
They're mean and low and cheap
And though they lead an upright life
Or dabble much in crime,
Though few make money and the rest
Lose their last thin dime,
They should sleep easier to know
No matter what nor who
Some readers blame you if you don't
And others if you do.

CHIN UP

It isn't everyone who can
Smile easily and say
The sun is bright, the world is right
I'm feeling fine today
Far easier to moan a bit
From heat bumps or a chill
And pass along to those you meet
The history of your ill.
Far easier to make complaint

And say the world is wrong
That justice is forgotten and
The race is to the strong
But this can only dim the smiles
Of self and all you meet,
And open hearts that once were light
To misery and defeat
So hide away your petty ills,
Your neighbors have them too;
Once out of sight is out of mind
With most that bothers you.

NATIONALISM

We build the pentagon and then
For dear old U.S.A.
We boast the biggest building and
We proudly point and say
No other country in the world
Can quite so proudly claim
Et cetera, et cetera
As on and on we name
Our huge resources as to size
Our bounteous wealth untold
From virgin ore and water power
To Fort Knox with its gold.
We're not braggarts, but we want
The best all for our own,
Then having topped the world we would
Quite loudly make it known
But all this shuns the well-known fact
Which may decide our fate;
Mere bigness as to wealth or size
Will not make nations great.

LONELINESS

The yearning of a lonely heart
Some people never know;
They make new friends and find new life
Wherever they may go.
But if some other souls should drift
Away from what they've known
They stay forever far apart
Disconsolate, alone;
The madding crowd may hurry by
Elbowing them aside.
But loneliness comes from within
And will not be denied.
Small matter then the laughter and
The outward joy of life
If loneliness is in your heart
And cuts through like a knife.

NEW YEAR

Why must the New Year always be
Brought forth in swaddling clothes,
An infant fair with ruddy cheek
And cuddly pink-shelled toes,
Or as a sheaf of pages white
All bound into a book
Where mortals may from day to day
Take a fateful look.
Might just as well this New Year be
Our friends, some new success,
The laughter of our children, or
A loved one's tenderness
Might just as well from yesteryear
We take the good, the glad.
And make these brief todays into
The best New Year we've had.

DELUDED MAN

The farthest reach of man's desire
Can never grasp the stars,
The feeble searching of the mind
Becomes our prison bars
That hold us fast within this sphere
Where we have been enslaved
By science, war-mad, conscienceless
And soulless men, depraved,
For while at heart we say we seek
The good and perfect life,
Our souls grow cold from war and hate,
Our blood flows out in strife;
And though we make an effort to
Feed those whom we have fought
We stop to argue back and forth
And wonder if we ought,
So let's hope God can overlook
This utter madness when
He calls us not Americans
But judges us as men.

ONE WORLD—LOST

Today our world is overcast
With deep'ning fearful gloom;
There is no sun, the stars are gone
No fragrant flowers bloom.
Our carefree days of yesterday
Are but a memory
When valiant men in battle song
Proclaimed the brave, the free.
Peace is a mocking, hollow shell,
Her great halls torn apart
By rocket's roar and atom bombs
That sear the human heart.
Where has fled our quiet peace

You ask, but none will say,
While lost in bickering and strife
We spend our empty day.

BIG SHOT

Some people splash their way through life,
You see them come and go
While others pull a deeper draft
And scarcely make a show
But you can rest assured that he
Who throws most foam and spray
Who elbows everything aside
Indiscriminately
And who is such a big shot if
You judge him by his sound
Or by the way he struts and brags
And throws his weight around
Is shallow in capacity
With mediocre brain
And scarcely knows which way to turn
To come in from the rain
He gets from life a battered head
From constant bout with fate,
Because he has no balance and
Cannot equilibrate.

REASON

Some folk see a man in the moon
And other folk declare
They see a lady there instead
With long and lovely hair.
Still others will not even look
Though looking be for free;
They say it's all a question of
Which one you want to see

So last night I observed quite well
And truthfully I say
There is a woman in the moon
Who will not go away,
But that is not the whole truth quite
So I must tell you true
The reason she is up there is
A man is up there too.

JUST A BOY

Bright-eyed, mischievous, dirty-faced
Snaggle-toothed and grinning
Clothes askew, white hair displaced
Band aids for underpinning,
Impudence mixed in tenderness
A bent for tricky toys
Constant look of ants in pants
Incessant, raucous noise
All bundled in a powder keg
With cream nuts, bubble gum
Or podded peppers, for to see
Would mean he'd bite off some
It totals up to one grand mess
Just plain as plain can be
But, no, I cannot sell him; so
He's still my Jamie Lee.

DESIRE

Our copybooks remind us that
The things we most desire
When once attained so often are
The things of which we tire
So quickly that the effort spent
Was wasted quite and so
We all should behave differently

When once this fact we know
But take away our keen desire
For things today can't reach
and we are scarcely more than just
Dead driftwood on the beach
Desire is that which motivates
An urge to go achieve
An alchemy of cleansing fire
A something to retrieve
From all today's deep sorrows
The will to live and grope
Down through our dim tomorrows
With dread, but constant hope.

WAY OF LIFE

Some people like to organize
And think to bypass strife
By stacking days like rows of brick
Into an ordered life.
Each small detail must fit just so
Each moment must be measured
So that in terms of minted gold
The memory may be treasured.
But others worry not a whit
And sing Life's way along
With happiness for all who care
To join them in the song
Until at last the two roads meet
Somewhere 'neath Western sun
Where all roads lead to earth and dust
And faith alone has won.

NEW CAR

My cousin likes a turn down top
With automatic door

And leather seats and spotlight and
New fangled fads galore.
My uncle wants a sleek sedan
Finished in solid black
With spacious doors for entrance both
In front and at the back.
My traveling salesman neighbor says
The tudor is his pick,
That with his many traveling chores
It really does the trick.
My groceryman says give to him
The half ton pick-up truck
But I have made no such request
And beg of Lady Luck
To go to some good dealer, please
Where all these others gripe
And whisper to him that I'll take
A red one, any type.

KNOW-HOW

As a child I always went
To watch the high trapeze;
I thrilled to see the acrobat
Fly through the air with ease.
I would haunt the blacksmith shop,
Watch carpenters at work,
And then rush home that very day
And labor like a Turk
To duplicate the easy tricks
That I had seen them do
But usually I must confess
My successes were few.
Since then I've seen the world's best
Of craftsmen ply their trade;
A few swift minutes with their hands
And lo! the thing is made,
But then I never could have known

What well I realize now
All things are easy if you spend
Enough years learning how!

HOLIDAY

I like to pack a bit of lunch
And seek some river's brink
Where thickets crowd close to its edge
And wild things come to drink.
There let me take the quietest spot
Beneath this thick-leaved shade
And call it my Allodium
And if per-chance you've strayed
Too far away and find yourself
Outside such opened door
Don't knock and ask if I am there
Or if there's room for more
But enter in and share with me
You're welcome, please be sure
For just as long as rivers run
Or sands and time endure.

IMMORTALITY

There is no end, no final goal
For just an earthly life,
No stopping place that satisfies
And calls an end to strife.
Each day is lived in hope of what
Tomorrow well can bring,
But that achievement comes and we
Find it was not the thing,
So on we grope eternally
Amid our world of fears
Till hope grows dim and stout hearts break
From frost of countless years,

But all this while within us lies
The secret, Life's real goal
All withered from disuse but still
An all immortal soul
Life's ups and downs take not away
Nor death its ties can sever;
We simply store within it Life
And Life is ours forever.

SICK

Oh, how I hate to go to bed
Though Doctor says I must
And even then it's only when
He's fumed and fussed and fussed
Until, at last, my family
Rise up and side with him
Then I'm tucked up to my chin
And sat upon with vim.
Of bitter potions I partake,
With stuff they grease my chest;
With heating pad I squirm and turn
Cause Doctor says its best
But by and by I cannot stand
This torture anymore
So stealthily I sit up and
Sneak out an unwatched door
And pronto! why I'm good as new
I breathe the open air
And find I got quite well despite
Doc's pills and coddling care.

SLACKS

Those women who prefer their slacks
Prefer them without doubt

And give no thought to what I think
Or dare to write about,
And I am sure they know full well
What styles suit just their size
So this is not meant to object
Or roundly criticize
It's just that when I see some pass
I'm puzzled I'll admit
By how far off somehow their slacks
Have missed the perfect fit.
The tailor's art may stand superb
When the Miss I'm meeting
But then in just one backward look
Be it ever fleeting
I know without a doubt that though
To say so wins few friends,
The jeans will not in every case
Quite justify the ends.

MUSIC

I think I'll learn to toot a horn
Or blow a bass bassoon
Or play the flute, or anything
Just so it makes a tune,
For studies show down through the years
In crime's bold rendition
Rarely will you ever find
Even one musician
So I've made plans to play the harp
Or try the big French horn
Even though the neighbors say
My playing is pure corn,
For in this way the sheriffs' men
May leave me playing yet
Instead of packing me away
To some far Joliet

Where thousands line the close locked cells
To music's charms immune
For in that legion of bad men
Not one can play a tune.

LAZY TRADER

Life has a friendly character
In each community;
Some fellow with a happy knack
Of tradeability.
He makes no effort that we see
And yet from day to day
An endless and a varied lot
Of bargains go his way
So even if we turn him out
With nothing but his wit
It would just put the rabbit in
The briar patch—he would sit
Quite unconcerned beside the way
And never bat an eye
The while he sold the river bridge
To all who happened by;
But wisely Nature placed his ease
Before gold or barter
Which means the rest of us wear shirts
Though he is much smarter.

MEMORIES

Some things come special in our lives
Their memory we treasure
And live again and once again
Each moment's brimming pleasure.

Perhaps some pain was in our song
For Time can never wait
While Destiny impatient stands
To hand us to our fate,
But on through life we can't forget
The pleasures or the pains
Until at last they blend as one
And joy alone remains,
So do we now recall the day
We lost a baby tooth
Or stubbed a toe in reckless play
In some far distant youth
So do we think of birthdays or
Striped sticks of peppermint,
Or glorious colors in the sky
From fireworks long since spent
And so our memories become
As paintings through the years
Gaily tinted from our songs
And drab sometimes from tears.

THANKSGIVING

Somehow this day has drifted from
Its meaning of the past
When sturdy forebears searched the wood
And faced the wint'ry blast
In search of turkey or marsh hen
So that their festive board
Could boast variety, and so
Their fruits of labor stored
Would last, with utmost frugal care
Perhaps the long year through
Though savages or pestilence
Could end it all, they knew
Today our food is all in tins.

Hunting is all for fun,
And God would be hard put to find
Accomplishments we've done,
So has our Thanksgiving gone stale
We're overblessed with much;
Civilization makes us soft
We've lost our humble touch,
And God could bless more richly if
Our wants did not exceed
With such a magnitude the things
That actually we need.

THE SAVERS

The wine in the bottle as yet untasted
Is only being saved. It is not wasted.
More important occasions may soon appear.
Tomorrow could bring to us moments more dear.

As apples we want are on branches too high,
We cannot reach so we pass them on by,
Time soon will mellow and they'll fall at our feet,
Our waiting only made them tender and sweet.

Life's moments withheld draw closer the spirit.
A being not touched can still feel you near it.
So patient the heart and free be the spirit.
From far, far away Love still hovers near it.

Now what of the bottle we savored and saved?
Too soon our free spirits, unfettered, unslaved,
Will leave to Unknowing this fine savored wine.
No longer will it be just yours and mine.

Should we then have saved such a wonderful wine?
Scruffy Unknowings may not think it so fine.

And as Time moves along, always the puzzle,
We save,
          We savor,
                    Unknowings guzzle.

So what of that wine
   We savored and saved?
Too soon our spirits,
   Abruptly unslaved,
Will let some Unknowing
   Open that sweet wine—
No more will it be
   Only yours and mine.

Should we then have saved
   Such wonderful wine?
Hell No! Unknowings
   May not think it fine!
Then our wine ends up
   An unsolved puzzle—
We planned to savor,
   Others will guzzle!

DILEMMA

The salesman said, "*Lady,*
I'll save you fifty bucks!"
Quickly she retorted.
"I just can't do it! Shucks!
We're saving near to forty
On our brand-new freezer;
All these gadgets help me
Plan my Life of Leisure;
Your washer fits real nice
In that corner,
But when I budgeted
I found, like Jack Horner,

If I put money in
I can't pull it out;
I'm so full up *saving*
I've got the *money gout.*

I know it sounds funny
But saving any more
Will cost so much, *paid out*
I'd be bankrupt once more!"

ARE AD MEN FAKIRS?

AD Men sure are funny
When they lay out their ads;
What they want is money,
Just scads and scads and scads.

They rack up us dummies
Like pool balls lacking brain;

Claim ninety per cent off,
And print it big and plain.

But then we need to know
Ninety from off of what?
Other ways, a license to steal
Is really what they've got!

Assume $100. were old price,
Ninety off leaves $10.
That could not buy the goods,
Pay profit, overhead,
From just that ten dollars—
To know the deal is bad wrong
Takes no band of scholars!

TOAST

May the Sun Gods touch thee tenderly,
May the Wind God set safe sail!
   May the God of all
   Keep you straight and tall
As you travel Life's long trail.

     We sleep and Time's soft lullaby
      Takes away our sorrow.
     Promises to us long since made
     Will still be ours tomorrow.

May your moccasins last through
many snows, and the Songbird of
Happiness build her nest near
your door.

     Too far gone? Too old! Ah, gee!
     Come on, Doc! Please work on me!

Make happy tracks on the
                  mudflats of Life,
Get your feet to the hills above!
There may you find peace, sucease
                  from strife,
And beneath some full moon a new love.

                        Should you chance on Magic Woods
                        Try not to hurry.
                        If slow you go
                        When deep the snow
                        Enjoy! Do not worry!

COLLEGE ISN'T EVERYTHING

Some things are by degree, others are not;
You may not know exactly what.
But this I think, whatever be said,
Intellect alone will make a cold bed.

THE LITTLE CROCUS KNOWS

In a spring of far existence lay a Crocus, under ground;
All at once, with quiet assurance, said the Crocus,
    "Sh-h! That sound!
Something goes on up there above us, above us on the ground.
I can hear the bright sun shining, playing whirlwind in the
    leaves;
Some small clouds are playing tag.
                        Who now among us but believes
That Spring is here, right up above us, raking last year's
    leaves."

"Wake up! Push up!" sang the Crocus, "Let earth not
    surround!"

"It is time" cried all the Croci, "let us push up and abound;
With our little tips of saffron, let us break the ground!"
So heaved they all a mighty *gro-w-w,* quietly herbaceous,
Till there they stood, exclaiming *Oh-h,* so very iridaceous,
With grasslike leaves, bulbous stems and their tiny blooms.

Gracéous!

"It's so early!" wailed the chorus of one million Crocuses;
"And where is Spring?" cried one wee Crocus, "Where is that
    playful breeze?"
Then all the Croci wept for spring, asking for the breeze,
    peeking under trees.
"Are we brothers? Are we cousins?" asked one Crocus, lone
    and white;
"No, I'm purple," said another, "and I'm saffron!"

Quite a sight,
As on they went, giggling and whispering, far into the night.
Bloom well, my little Crocuses!

Good night.

Sleep tight!

RAINBOW SNATCHER

I caught a small child's laugh today, on first bounce, as it
    started.
Soon I had picked a wanton breeze and wore it, open-hearted.
I dipped a lake off dry land, but arms could not quite reach
So I scooped up the golden sand along a sun-lit beach.

I shook a wood with shouts of glee till Echoes came to dance;
Small birds and foxes looked at me, all quizzically askance.
I speared a rainbow as I ran, and had myself great fun—
But rainbows end as they began when once you've lost the sun.

THE DOGWOOD

When seasons pulse anew with life I always get a thrill
To see the dogwood, pink and white, come marching up my
    hill.
Like a calendar, like notching a stick, I count slow time
By this marching color band, who with rhythm and with
    rhyme
Seem intent, like well-trained troops, to take each fence and
    clearing,
While to every bush below another is adhering.

Cut one down? I never could, though in my path 'twere
    standing.
It will surely break my heart if dogwood start disbanding.
I know that other trees, in size, John Bunyan would delight,
But let us plant more dogwood
                    Till the woods are pink and white.

CITY OF THE MILLION LIGHTS

O City of the Million Lights, you proudly raised
    your head
And said, "Behold my wond'rous sights"; I looked
    and saw instead

A starved youngster come to buy, where millions
    daily strive;
He humbly offered pennies four; you sent him
    back for five.

I saw your Christmas fires burn bright. Outside
    was snow and sleet,
But numb and frozen through this night, an old
    man walked your street.

I saw your women slink the streets, bold-eyed and
full of breast;
I heard your bad men make their boast, your roaring dives infest.

O City of the Million Lights, I heard your racing
cars.
Your children see your wond'rous sights. Have they
seen the stars?

O City of the Million Lights, you proudly raised
your head
And bade me gaze upon your sights. These I saw
instead.

PRAYER

Just a bit backside of heaven—ah, there could be my place. Let it face the West, but not too much sun in my face. Make it leaf-latticed, with a faint smell of violets, like some deep mountain glade.

Give me a clump of moss to hold my halo, and one big rhododendron bush on which to spread my wings.

If heaven can manage a few hills and one tall mountain with backside for a garden, come the close of my day, I'll think You, Lord.

I won't need the golden key.

THE THIN ICE

Escape is rare. Count not that twice
The gods will squeak you by.
You watch your step on that thin ice;
Flaunt not a falling sky.

To hell with sly banana peels,
  Ladders sail right under;
Go fly a kite—know how it feels
  To play tag with thunder.

The surgeon will be very nice,
  The nurses sweet as pie—
But lightly, Sir, on the thin ice,
  And watch that falling sky.

SAY THAT AGAIN

If God had pushed the buttons right
  On his great computer,
He might have made a perfect Eve,
  One maybe even cuter!
And Adam still could have his rib
  Some claim the woman's using;
But by my count the rib grew back—
  It really is confusing!

EARLY SPRING

It's a beautiful day . . . sky azure blue . . .
  Red robins picketing the lawn . . .
A perfect day for thinking of you,
  And the winter seeming gone.

But thousands of robins skipping about,
  Or a hundred skies above,
Don't balance out when I do without
  The wonderful one I love.

SONG OF SONGS

Some songs cry to the winds, some songs
    Whimper away the night;
Some songs soothe away all wrongs,
    To set the world aright.
Some songs sing to the soul, some songs
    Are much too sad for singing;
But yours to me are as great throngs
    Who joy to me keep bringing.

WISHING WELL

February took my hand
    In fingers shivered gray.
I wished instead for flowers and sun;
    Oh, how I wished for May.

But while time stood, or so I thought,
    And spring was but a dream,
I saw one day a robin stand
    Beside a thawing stream.

And soon the willow buds had burst
    Where sun fell warm and sweet,
For March had taken me to May
    On April's winged feet.

THE KILLING FIELD

Long flat temple, ribbon endless
    Winding through my day;
Asphalt, concrete, cold and friendless,
    Stretching far away.

The sacred chromed-snout herds fume cud,
   Trumpet, blare and screech
For human sacrifice now stood
   Curbside, out of reach.

Bright ruby red
Above the square,
Changing now to green,
Your idol's head
Is swinging there
In ambered sheen
To wink and bid your futile price:
More human sacrifice.

The victim pauses, does not think,
Darts right in at first quick wink.
One screeching thrust from the hurtling high priest
Fells him. He retches red,
Head
Bashed like a crushed rat
Waiting lonely, gurgling death
In your dirty gutters.

Tomorrow's offering pauses.
Nauseas
Sweep him, but in a moment
He hurries on, nor mutters
At his impending fate.

Once more your high priest of state
Has called his sacred chrome-finned herds
To trample your templed altars;
They fill your dirty gutters;
They furnish fresh cadaver,
Hard, choked-up, tearless words,
And tight new hate.

THE CACHE

A Fable Of Finite Man

Tvastri searched and found the leak.
It had been cleverly put there by some bellicose spirit,
Slow and direct from the innards of hell.

Tvastri knew it was spreading its corrosive poisons deep
    into his mountains, and seeping through his valleys
    to spoil the good green earth which he had reserved
    for man.
So Tvastri sealed it off and covered it deep, scattering its
    elements thither and yon.
He set tall mountains over it, under massive groves of
    balsam and fir, and thought he had hidden well.

Tvastri reckoned without man, who was then in the
    springtime of his existence, and filled with a curious
    seeking.
This man was at once possessed with the cleverness of a
    demon and the meekness of a little boy.
His was a relentless driving force, forever pouring intellect
    into more powerful space capsules to press ever closer
    against the very windows of heaven, or forcing grimy,
    geophysical fingers deeper into the terrestial cookie
    jar.

As man moved nearer heaven's base, or probed deeper into
    the dark earth, he was fascinated by a strange, haunting
    iridescence. It was the long-last tracing left by this
    weirdly-beautiful, once divinely hidden, seepage.

Feverish with the import of his discovery, man isolated
    these elements and jig-sawed them back together.
What he found he nurtured and made it to come alive.

In the image of his Creator, and being a child of the
      Omnipotence, man none the less possessed a certain
      predisposition to disobey.
This now began to assert itself.

Man pondered deeply what he had found, but he told no
      one.

Alas, he had stumbled on Tvastri's power of the planned
      universe, blindly and unprepared; nor had he unraveled
      the creative magic that lay within; only its thunder
      and destruction.

Man grew furtive and secretive.
He hugged this terrible thing to his bosom, greedy in
      possession, fearing it might be wrested from him.

Like a strange, poisonous flower
Found by the little child who chews upon it
And dies,
So man was drawn irresistibly to close his fingers upon this
      thing.

Soon man was loudly demanding that mudballs be made
      of his secret discovery, saying that he needed to store
      them away for possible future emergency; before long
      he tossed two of them broadside at one of his more
      disliked neighbors, being greatly sobered by what he
      saw.
But not for long.

Man decided that he would now roll everything into one
      great mudball, wrap his fingers firmly about it, and
      squeeze tightly. He would see, and scientifically
      record, what happened. Perhaps he would find the
      secret of life itself.
Just then Tvastri decided it was time. He reached tenderly
      to touch man's heart, and warmed it to new concepts
      of peace.

Reasoning within himself, man concluded that his new
understanding must be coming from the mudballs he
had made, because he had not known that Tvastri
touched him.

Perhaps this was better, for man soon joined with his
neighbors, who incidentally were also learning to
make mudballs, and presently they had all agreed to
banish mudball-making forever.

FOUR POEMS ON HERCULES

HERCULES AND THE WHISTLING WIND

A wind is rising. Sea caps show their white teeth.
    Listen!
The sea nymph's far-off murmuring splashes proud ears,
    fast firms the soft-fuzzed face.

Blow, Day! Go scampering, kittenish Dawn.
Play, Pipes. Not softly, but with the rising wind.

Something cuts through this taut rigging like a white-hot knife.
The boil of hot blood, gurgling, has no ebb;
Strange masts, unsailed, are bucking to be tried.

Up anchor, Lad. Set full sail.
Push off. Find new warm sun.
There comes the day, too quickly,
When whistling winds are done.

HERCULES HOME

Mark this, the dark voyage comes at last to its shore.
I am tired of storm-tossed passage, of lonely sailing;
Oh, make me to search no more.

As of Time's beginning the sperm forth seeking ovum
Upward through darkness finds it life,
Searching, reaching, forming, keeping
For infinite soul a temporal shell.
Then journey back, dark passage to light, warmth, love—
But not quite, not yet to ending;
Still it must seek
                Like homing dove
Who leaves ark mother to search on and on,
Unrequired, lost, alone,
Caught between Ten Commandments and flood of the
    godless,
Cleaving to nothing that is man's own,
To harbor at last into cradling arms,
Head against succoring breast,
Fingers caressing, soft voice inviting
Welcome peaceful rest.

Oh, bid me to stay, let this be my home,
As the harbor snugs to its shore;
Oh, love me too much to leave me to roam,
For I would stray no more.

HERCULES CHAINED TO OBLIVION

Wrapped in a great tenderness I have borne you away.
On this oarless galleon of the ceaseless mind you are my
    prisoner.

But, alas,
Since first I drank of the forgetful warers of Lethe,
Leaving you, my beloved Hebe, lips untouched, arms empty,
and
The fires of Pheglethon unquenched,
So very much I have sinned.

It is becuase I cover you; because I cannot possess.
Each night I reach my arms, while the distant heavens
crackle their forked lightnings of an all-consuming desire,
But when at last you come to me you are sheathed as a
shadow etched in emptiness;
And gladly I drink again of Lethe's oblivioned waters,
poured and set to me by some malevolent, jealous god.
Then woe for me.
I would again to the open sea, where sharp salt spray shall
ease this fevered brow.
But that cannot be;
So in the remembered forgetfulness of these sparkling
waters where never we should have met, but first I
slaked my thirst, I will abide.

From this far jut of lonely shore, each time I see Orion
striding across the still-free heavens,
Sword in hand, profaning the fair meadows of the gods in
his mad search for thee,
I shall cry out in remembering, and rattle my chains in
helpless anger,
And long O Hebe but for thee.

REGRET

Speak no more of love in spring;
bring no wine on quick bare feet, nor
ask of me to drink—for spent is the
summer of Hercules, leaving an old man
only his forgetting.

Now Love lies heavy beside him,
    eternity sleep-leaden in her fallen breasts;
    nor can ever another spring, even in memory,
    press such strong wine from these shriveled
    grapes as to raise one last gambol for the fall.

THE TWELVE SONS OF SAM

I

From a cliff in the Appalachian on the Smokies' Southmost
    side
Where the eaglets pause, come summer, and in winter
    black bear hide,
There's a cleft in the rock whence the Deep Creek flows,
Fed fat from the peaks of the thousand snows.

It's North of the Nantahala, North by West two suns,
Across a meadowed valley where the Tuckaseegee runs,
On up the Oconaluftee beyond the Cherokee—
Here was born a man who had twelve sons.
                        His name was Sam. Now he
Was a peaceable man and a hunter.
                        Sam
Just prowled and fished.
                        He didn't give a damn
How much of this steel some John Henry drove,
Or how much roving old Paul Bunyan rove,
Or how much steak you could take from Bunyan's ox,
While his ears could feast on his hounds and a fox.

On history you might say Sam wasn't much punkin—
Never heard of the Maine nor the bay she was sunk in.
Thought Cornwallis was a new kind of corn,
And Brandywine? Why the day Sam was born
He sat right up on his Mammy's knee,
Smoked Granny's pipe, cute as could be,
Then snitched Pa's jug and took him a swig.
Sam was quiet, all right, but he *thought* big!

Sam had big gnarled hands, square jaw, jutting chin,
White teeth, black beard, and a twisted grin
That curled about like mountain smoke, come lazy
    autumn days
When the mountain peaks r'ar way back and lose
    themselves in haze.

Sam could never be called a Dandy Dan,
Nor a scholar yet, but a gentle man,
And a way with a dog he had, or a maid—
Sam treated both alike, and both obeyed
With a worshipful look and eye unbowed.
You could tell, dog or maid, each felt right proud
To know Big Sam with his jutting chin,
Big ears, blue eyes and winsome grin.

II

Turned six Big Sam started out to school,
Made friends with his teacher, obeyed every rule.
And though as he grew waistcoat never spoiled him,
He became more mannerly, few things roiled him.

Sam was tender.
               That first year, one cool fall day,
He took the pasture path; it was quicker that way;
There beneath an old oak a cow and calf lay.
A mere lad of six, what would Sam do now?
This calf could still walk—Sam carried the cow!

III

As Sam grew older each day's need
Seemed quite sufficient. Hurry and greed
Had none of Sam. They were not in his book,
Nor was there a man who, taking his look
At Big Sam, Mountain Man, could more doubt

That here was a man who went about
This business of living as any man should
Who had promised a loving mother he would.

And so it went.
                    There isn't much story.
Sam split rail, fenced, framed, hunted in glory.
Sam grew older, married, had children twelve,
Like stair steps, from giant to stray little elve—
You'll find them now, from Cherokee
To the banks of the Little Tennessee;
From Clingman's Dome to Nantahala Gorge—
Some known as Frank, some Jim, some George.

And father to son in this mountain clan,
As generations pass, each is the man
Of a mountain tradition he has known
Since the day Mountain Sam, six and alone,
Defined his own duty beneath that oak's bough,
And let a calf walk while he carried a cow.

Let soft modern man to his small burdens bow,
But the twelve sons of Sam still carry the cow.

Note: This was first published in Falling Sky, *1961. The world was different then!*

Just forty short years ago if you said that the moon is made of green cheese, who could prove you wrong? Also, everybody was building bomb shelters because of The Russian Bear.

What a difference a few years make. The Bear is now housebroken, and China starts to growl. We've been to the moon, we're playing tag with the genetic code, and the more questions we answer, the longer the list we ask.

The Falling Sky, written in the fifties and first published in 1961, was pure imagination, mixed with a few Greek Classics sprinkled with the thoughts of a midget thinker who walks out, small boy like, looks at the world about him, and thinks aloud "Oh, My God!"

The more we learn, the more we realize that we really don't know much at all, even about this incredibly complex shell of a body we live in here on earth. Columbus sailed, but he had no chart to identify his destination. Today, as then, transient man launches his ship on the trackless ocean of Time, unknown, uncharted. And Time doesn't pass; man passes. Like Columbus, we know where we start (if not why), but Faith, Belief, and man's ever-widening scrap of knowledge, are the only charts by which we sail.

THE FALLING SKY

A Space-Age Fable in Three Parts

PROLOGUE

The Fortune Teller stirred her tea,
And stirred and stirred, then said to me
"No matter how the brew I stir,
Your sky still falls, O most kind Sir!"

The Old Hag was right! Don't laugh; you wait and see!
Some day broken, jagged sky may tumble down on thee!

It won't be any one thing, like
    unions, Russians, tax collectors, astronauts,
    neighborhood dogs, H-bomb blasts, nor even a
    barb-wire fence and your new blue serge, should
    some Ferdinand sneak up on thee.
It may be another thing.
                O Brother, can your Mad Fates
                go on a spree!

Each finds his own.
             I lost the decision
To a wife, four kids, and Television!

Mine was a blunt approach, ill-fated, do not doubt;
TV offended, and
            I thought to kick it out.

Then, like Brer Rabbit who slapped the Tar Baby, or
    Jonah, swallowed up by his whale,
I was tricked by this thing, this Monster, TV—
Judge not, but I pray, as you read may you see how to
    profit from my sad tale.

PART ONE

BLAST OFF!

*The moral is the first business of the poet; this being
formed, he contrives such a design of fable as may be most
suitable to the moral.*

                                  —*Dryden*

HOW IT BEGAN

I was reading the book daughter Ann
Brought home from school for her lesson plan.
Three Gorgon sisters, horse on a steeple—
Ha! Those Greeks were the craziest people!

But reading the Greek Mythology
Could never have forced this thing on me.
The ball started bouncing, doctors said,
When the antenna fell on my head.

I remember now.
                            There climbed I
Two mast-poles up, a human fly—
With great gleeful case
I pulled down wire till my crazy trapeze
Of a wife-held ladder slipped and rolled—
"Water!" she screamed loudly, "He's out cold!"

My head oozed blood;
                        The merry-go-round
I tried to clutch was the hard, cold ground.
The falling antenna had pierced my brain;
My doctor said at once it would have to remain.

PAY-OFF

With TV gone all should have been well.
But I heard *klop, klop,* clear as a bell.
I could dimly see a horse, *with wings.*
                              He brayed and acted gay.
The picture stuck like lint to serge from that first sad day.

Could I be by myself? Why, heck, no;
Like Mary's little lamb, that *horse* had to go.

Pulling on my boot, he was the burr;
If I tried to sleep, he thought to stir;
When I sought peace, he was troubled;
What Job endured, this horse doubled.

So you Wall Markers mark this case double—
Trying to run is causing our trouble!

MISTAKE NUMBER TWO

Before wising up how dumb can one get!
This mule-eared Horse Thing could talk to me yet.

Jesting I dared his sorcery;
What happened you'll shudder to see:

If a horse grow wings, I sneered, so I can;
Hah! Make me to orbit, a real Space Man.

Too late!
         I had wished.
                        I felt these things
Sprouting, pushing,
                    Like two tiny wings!

They were stubby and weak and short. Oh, dear!
But the Horse said proudly, "Your wings are here!"

NOW WHOA IS ME!

My brain aches from clanking of spurs,
And whirring wings and cockleburs.

I'm a sick man, but I can't lie in bed
With this antenna stuck right through my head.

If that hasn't done it, of all things
I've sprouted these damned, gosh-awful wings!

BARELY HANGING ON

Steady, Lad.
         Such ancient love
Is storybook fable, nothing more.
Your horse is a joke.
            You are still able
To think clearly. He is fable.
Sure you're sure!
          Sit at this table
And explain the winged horse.
                 He is fable.

Perseus, son of Zeus, by an ancient sea
Slew Medusa of the Gorgon Three.
This was the Greek.
          Mythology
Is just a fairy book. Ah, you see!
This horse's birth by the sword can be
Nothing but a trumped-up mystery.

Oh, of course there is fascination
In reading his story. Your elation
Has grown to learn of Pegasus's wings;
His strange powers with poets and things.
You like the fine horse.
              His cloud-like spirit
Gives you a lift; you like to be near it.

But antennas? Wings? Come now, confess;
There's no reasoning all that mess!

SLOWLY LOSING GRIP

The dream persisted. Eventually
I began to wonder. Would it be
That I could never, never dare
To rid myself of his nightmare?

Ever harder I struggled to rid,
But stronger, stronger the winged horse bid.

Fascinated I reread mythology:
How those fearful Gorgon sisters numbered three;
Of them, Madusa was the only mortal—
And now, close by, I heard a soft, low chortle.

Of all the utterly silly things!
Antennas, Gorgons, now these damned wings!

I would come clean.
                    The thing had me;
And sisters Stheno and Euryale,
Through a daring bit of deviltry,
Were trying to take me, don't you see,
With their fatal frozen statuary?

Things came clearer, minute by minute.
Medusa's masterpiece?
                        Lord, I was in it!

I pictured the snakes coiled in her hair;
I expected, turning, to find her there.
I slept fully clothed, taking due care
That turned to stone I shouldn't be bare!
Atlas-like I could be a mountain.
Who wanted eternity filling a fountain!

RETREAT

I

As a Man thinketh, so is he.
Really, I suppose, that explains me.

On Soul's oceans I fought to the beaches;
In the Mind's forests and from the black reaches
And jungled recesses where thought-rivers head
I stoutly resisted.
                    My tumbled bed
Each morning showed new battle grounds
Where by night low hissing sounds
Of Gorgon snakes that petrified men
Made of my coverlets one dark den
Of cowering fear.
                    Mornings found me
Dreaming fitfully of statuary.

II

Running from Fate sounds quite on the level;
Long be your flight, but sure as the devil
What is to be shall be.
                    By the stars
There's little to gain from battle scars
That needn't have been if one had quit
With enough sense yet to think of it!

III

Fear spurred me on to stem this tide;
Not courage, not bravery, just saving my hide.

This was it. I would furl my flags.
All right, Pegasus!
                    Where are those hags?

IV

Silence.

      The chilling nightmare of quiet;
A kick of the monkey in ghoulish riot;
The void of emptiness covered me
On a barren beach by a glassy sea.

The crescendo of nothing filled my night.
No sound—just fever and sickening fright.

PART TWO

LONG GONE!

*A fading vapor trail no more
Marks from the sea Canaveral's shore.*

*Low earthly haze that clouds the mind
Is all that's left.*
         *We never find
Quite all the parts or where they fit.
Life is short when we've lost it.*

THE ABYSS

"Ha, Pig Eyes, you'll never find me!"
Hissed old Stheno just behind me.
"Scribble away; but on this make book—
Your Fates have spoken; you cannot look.

"They've said you are so very fat you
Would not make a very good statue.
So blubber on, your avoirdupois
Keeps you, for now, just one of the boys.
But should you lose that extra gear lube
I shall make of you one big ice cube!

"Come, Old Morpheus, draper of drapes,
Prince of the Netherland, shaper of shapes;
To your keeping I entrust him.
Treat him rough.
                    May Pegasus bust him!

"Morpheus!
            Morpheus,
                        Dammit, be gone!
Hades waits. Take him on!"

DOWN THE STYX

I glimpsed Cerberus drowsily;
His three heads closed on me,
   Boxer, fice and hound.
All three heads barked angrily,
The river Styx roared fearfully,
   Though I could hear no sound.

Old Charon rowed us silently.
Pegasus trembled violently
As he jostled me around.
To Hades we were bound.

CRONUS BARS THE WAY

I

"Look," cried Pegasus, "there's old Cronus!"
A stooped old man was almost upon us.

Both shores of the Styx moved furiously;
In but a moment I was sure we
Would far outrun the spot where Cronus
Now just stood and looked upon us.

But Pegasus counseled, "No, not ever.
Overrun Time? We can never!
Time is illusion.
                    Look, I'll prove
That neither Time nor we can move!

"These banks that passing seem to be
Are the rims of two wheels.
                        You can't see,
But the Past moves left, the Future, right,
Almost meshing, though never quite.

"The spot where we stand is called the *Now,*
In between these two wheels.
                      That is how
We work and work but never progress
Beyond earthly hopelessness.
Just as we think we can't be losin',
Life has passed on Time's Lazy Susan.

II

Hope hangs her lantern, by which we
Through these shades think now we see
A harbor safe, so close we'll make it;
But we reach and reach; we never take it!

"This world," said Pegasus, "is on a treadmill;
And you, my Lad, are standing still,
As history stands to repeat, repeat
Where the rims of the two wheels never meet.

"Look to the outer edges of the wheels;
See those tall trees, those great green fields?
They're moving forward just as much as
These nearer rims, where the bank touches.
Are moving back to meet us here."

Fate's Machiavellian plan was clear.
I was trapped, as on Grecian Urn;

I was suspended, never to turn
My mortal shell from its rack;
I wasn't moving, to Hell or back!

<h3 style="text-align:center">III</h3>

Steep a soul in lonely yearning,
But lose the mind that has no turning.

So for this, deep within Time's wheels
Waves old Cronus, ready with deals,
Inexorable Fates, undaunted Furies,
Or sweet light Muses, just as sure as
His hands move round and round his face—
And always, Cronus wins his race.

<h3 style="text-align:center">IV</h3>

All life is circling, round and round
From the dust of the earth back to the ground
That opens at last again to enfold us;
Mother Earth alone then can hold us.

The Seasons circle, the Moon, the Sun,
The hands on the Time-Piece run and run;
And all things end as they began—
Moving out of orbit only is man!

For Man no finite sea nor shore,
    No far-off, fog-bound landing;
Time was and is, shall be the more
    Just where his Soul is standing.

<h2 style="text-align:center">MAN AND TIME</h2>

<h3 style="text-align:center">I</h3>

"Relax," said Pegasus, "you can trust me.
This is mind over matter.
                    You must see

That the eye of a Soul is the mind of the Man,
And that for you there is just this plan:

"Getting out of orbit is the one sure way
To outwit Cronus.
                     Otherwise you stay
Suspended in Space, fretting and proving
Sky may be falling, but you are not moving!

"Let Charon, boatman, son of darkness,
Beach you here and take the shell;
Save mind and soul, the eye and its body;
If you have saved them, all is well.

"No matter that Cronus pounds away,
Circling his circle, day on to day;
Far out of orbit you will be
In Elysian fields, eternally.
Time there is always.
                  You will be free!"

II

I rose rapidly, twisting, turning;
How good, how good to be free!
The Styx receded.
                Time's great wheels turning
No longer treadmilled me.
Detached now, I could see below
   Old Charon still afloat;
How he was pushing, rowing, pulling,
   Trying to beach my boat.

Clearly I could see the two great wheels
   That border the *Gorge of the Now;*
I could see Cronus turning those wheels,
   Struggling.
            I could see how,

Encased in the clay of the earthly,
    Fettered to my small groove,
I should never, barring old Gabe's horn,
    Have caused one foot to move!

PULPITIZING IN HADES

Inveriably this thing called Sin
Corrodes the molars, stains the chin,
Splatters the corners the spittoons are in.

Some is store-bought, some home-grown.
You'd be surprised the folks who're known
To go out and try to lip it
After watching experts dip it.

To tell the truth, this thing of Sin
Starts with the frame of mind you're in;
And ends corroding frames of steel,
Gumming dirt in the balance wheel;
Freezing many poor old porkers
Into statues that are corkers.

Come, let's take a little tour;
See for yourself, just to be sure.

See this famous Politician?
Names don't matter. Look, he's fishin'
In Simple Simon's empty pail.
He really thinks he'll catch a whale.
He spent his life lying, thieving;
Now his own lies he's believing.

Here is Sisyphus, Ulysses' father.
To him the eternal bother
Of rolling stones up yonder hill;
Hard though he tried, they roll down still.

Look at this one—mustachioed,
And short and squat and pigeon-toed.
The world he collared while he made
Them watch his goose-stepping parade.
But Hell took glitter back to shelf;
He goosesteps now but for himself.

Forgive, please, much moralizing,
But Hell still is tantalizing
Tantalus, the young king who snitched
On the seven Gods. He is ditched
Chin-deep in nectar, always athirst,
Below tall trees ready to burst
With fruits, and one huge rock to fall—
This is Tantalus' chain and ball.

Or see what Hell offers to wives
Who murder husbands with long knives:
Danaides, the forty-nine daughters,
Were condemned to pouring waters
In their sieves. They pour and pour,
But empty, empty calls for more.

The fiftieth daughter, Amymone,
Escaped this hell, for quietly she
Went to Argos in its need,
And was pardoned for her good deed.

Husband need knifing? Then Hell wait
While you stuff some collection plate,
And after that perhaps you'll say
"He quite deserved it, anyway!"

But please note: Hell hath no Furies
Who think like all-woman juries;
Nor can Hell first set its hook
If at Gorgon you won't look.

But if you look, you taste, you eat—
And then and there, Hell has you beat!

AT THE THRESHOLD

Said Pegasus, "I might have known!
To see Pluto we should have gone
Straight down to Cape Canaveral.
Come, Kind Sir, and let us travel."

Big signs read "Civilians Not Permitted,"
But Peg just laughed; in we flitted.
We were not civilians.
                    Mercy on us!
We were fugitives from Cronus.

Sprawled in the ready room, wild, red-eyed,
A score of Scientists we spied.
Spread out before them were no charts,
No space-ship innards, no spare parts,
No mechanical buzz-bomb hearts,
No smart monkeys like Baker and Able—
Just these old codgers pulled up to the table.

Loudspeakers crackled the long count-down;
Those Longhairs sat there, going to town
In one grim struggle for all to see,
Playing madly gin rummy for three!

LATER THAN WE THINK

"Come," said Pegasus, "Hell is spewing;
We have some things that need quick doing!
No gin rummy, no time for fun—
We must get back to Washington!"

Then "Hold it," Peg cried,
                      "Oh, Oh!
See Time's wheels zizz and go!
Polished and balanced, with cosmic springs,
These wheels truly are delicate things.

"And if some day our U.S.A.
Or Khrushchev shouts 'Bombs Away!'
They've pulled our last cosmic molar;
Earth will jump like a Rock 'n' Roller.

"And should this happen, like as not
Time's wheels will collide.
                              On the spot
We call the *Now*, between Time's wheels,
Where lie fair schools and pleasant fields,
Will spout Hades.
                              On Time's face
None can ever find this place.

PART THREE

RE-ENTRY

DILEMMA

The Cross remains a cross no more,
But a crossroad now;
                              Time's open door
Of lonely grave that man has known
Has space-age stars to lure him on
Through Hell's atomic flame—
How now, O Man, in heaven's name
Can you know the one sure way, or be
Certain where Eternity?

CROSSROADS

I

The Preacher stood on his velveted stair,
And etched above him clearly there
Were the cross-filled years of the Nazarene

217

In peaceful shadow.
                    All between
The tall-spired Cross and the River's Bend,
Where the good died young and those who sinned
Flourished on as the green bay tree,
The Preacher's message, reverently,
Fell on the thistle.
                    Men hungered for news,
But cold stained windows hid long-empty pews.

Simple and profound, for all to hear,
The Preacher preached, loud and clear:
The lame could walk, the blind would see,
In Christ's prepared Eternity;
Cast doubt, he pled, *shed mortal sin,*
Believe on him and enter in.

The Preacher, meek and long-beseeching,
Held forth to Man this

EASTER TEACHING:

Fall tulips planted in cold ground
With coming spring are always found.
Despite late frost and wintery chill
They break their bonds.
                    They always will.

Burial brings but new beginning;
This Man must learn.
                    His greatest sinning
Is starving Soul on solitaire
In a small mind.
                    That is where
Earth becomes his total prison—
Through Death alone has Man arisen.

If Death be the gateway, this be said:
Thanks to Death, there are no dead.

II

The Twentieth Shadow's ugly dross
Covered a fallen and broken Cross.
A being of Science, this huge Thing turned
Ever to Space.
    Man's mind burned
Bright as the stars; Man sought new teaching;
Man falconed his Soul, searching, reaching
Toward Saturn, Venus, Jupiter, Mars—
And out, on out to the nearer stars.

Attain speed of light! Mount Thought's fleet wing!
Full mastery of Space now became the thing
That Man most wanted.
    Like the Garden's fruit,
Man reached for everything, Space to boot.
The voice of The Shadow, rumbling, blasting,
Like an eviled Piper ever casting
Its fateful lure, said "Hail, Super Race!
All heaven waits, if you conquer Space!"

The substance of The Shadow's teaching
I here set forth in

MAN, STILL REACHING:

As flowers' fragrance comes of bloom,
So glory of Man is his living room,
And riding a Snark or a Jupiter-C
Man's reach improves immeasurably.

Old Mount Olympus fades far below,
And Hades gives but small red glow,
Like launching pads at Cape Canaveral,
Where glorious Man will unravel
All past and future from Time's two wheels,
But always is *Now*, when Eternity feels
Like the lightest, brightest, mid-May mornin'
That ever four billion souls were born in.

So despite all Heaven's trumpeting doom,
In Elysian fields fragrant with bloom
(It now seems a fact beyond assume)
Man, in Space, will find his room.

III

"No!

    Wait!"

        I cried,

            "Please, Dear God, forbid!"

Such a thing could not happen!

               But suppose it did!

If out in Space at the speed of light
Time stood still and nothing but night
Stretched out from his Spaceship, would no end,
Where could Man turn? Who would be his friend?

Would God call again in that fateful *Now,*
"Adam?

        O foolish Adam! Where art thou?"

The full horror came home to me.
What an awful punishment should we
Be flung through Space from Gravity's string
Forever and ever.

           Never to bring
Our Soulship back to its rightful glory—
How wild and screeching this purgatory
Of profaned atoms, wild banshee whistles
From Earth's runaway hydrogen missiles!

What a ghastly vision!

            Millions of dead
Scrambled, mutilated; not one head
To have among them, even an eye,
Nor an arm to reach with.

            Why, oh, why

Must we rush hell-bent in one mad race
To outer, infinite, vacuumed Space?

How does Man think to accomplish more
Tearing through Time's wall?
                              God made him a door!

True, speed of sound won Man's earth race,
But speed of light Man seeks in Space—
And moving light will stop the treadmill
Like a stroboscope.
                    Time's wheels will still.
Man will not age, nor can he die—
The grave was a door, but he passed it by!

Then all the vision I had wrought
Went floating off in wispy thought.

IV

Did Man through his grave escape perdition?
Did Man break Time?
                    The final edition,
Whether Canaveral, Mars or Venus,
Will not matter.
                Gabriel has seen us!

I recall this one thing:
                        The human race
Stood at its crossroad.
                        Out in Space
A night's stars twinkled, beckoning on—
But when I looked closer,
                        Man had gone!

EPILOGUE

Far above in my patch of sky
A few low clouds were floating by.

One cloud soon grew scraggly fat,
And I knew instinctively that
Here was the Pegasus I had met
And come to know as friend.

                              Yet
At this moment he was drifting away
Farther and farther.

                    The fading day
Tinged his flanks in pure spun gold;
His wings were drooped; he looked old.

Suddenly the Wind Gods purled new reins
To his tangled, tousled, sun-flecked manes;
Smoothly he pranced and galloped away
Toward the West's swift darkening day.

Now he slowed; gingerly he let
One front foot touch the gold sunset;
He disappeared in its brilliant flame;
Pegasus again was only a name.

Yet out of the mists, as the mornings clear,
My friend of much wisdom shall reappear.
When reading sometimes I shall catch a glint
Of his silvery mane, his trim hoof-print.

I shall know too well the sound of his wings,
His strange little whinny telling me things;
The siren effect of our haunting songs—
Pegasus will come back
                        Where he belongs.

THE TWO OF US

We dwell in one house
Brother to brother,
Yet one on the street
Knows not the other.

In fact, we are one
Which you can see
Makes for needed
Economy.

But his the passion;
I, content,
Labor on
To pay our rent.
His the vision;
I, instead,
Tend some furnace
To buy us bread.

MY APOLOGIES

To the man I might have been,
    The boy I used to be.
The boy is gone; and the man—
    Well, somehow, plain to see,
Fate just put me in his stead.
    So no one else be blamed
That a boy's dream went for bread
    And substance. How ashamed
I am; in the marketplace
    I've trafficked on like mad
Until this boy walked away
    From all the dream he had.

So, for him of yesteryear
    I now can do no worse;
I've gathered here his first love,
    His youthful dream, his verse.

That's the Way It Was

This story appeared in the Brevard College newspaper sometime in the early eighties. An alumnus was writing about his memory of "Professor Leroy Sossamon" and a lecture-demonstration he presented at the college in late spring, 1935.

Back in the Depression, 1934–35, when Brevard College came into existence, there was little money available for bringing cultural attractions to the campus. The desirability of doing so, however, was well recognized by Dr. Coltrane and the faculty. We had a few outside lecturers and various individual faculty members who also "did their thing." I remember the Cotton Blossom singers, students from a black college in Mississippi, singing spirituals; another glee club or two; and an ex-Metropolitan Opera singer who impressed us as much by her stylish, articulate stage appearance as by her voice.

But the outstanding attraction of that first year was Professor Leroy Sossamon, the Hypnotist. After 46 years (written in '81) my memory of this event is hazy as to some names and details, but many things I have never forgotten. As I remember, the "Professor" was a high school teacher somewhere in the state who put on his shows to earn a little extra money in those difficult times.

He was enterprising enough to have had some advance flyers sent to us and the local newspaper. In fact, the local paper announced that on the day of his show he would have a man under hypnosis, all day, lying in the window of the drugstore downtown. Several of us walked from Ross Hall to town to check this out and found it indeed true. There in the window was a man not only in a trance, but with a metal skewer running through his cheek. As you can imagine the word got out and nearly all of our 300-plus student body paid their admission and were in the auditorium at 8:00 p.m. showtime.

There were and, I expect, still are many charlatan hypnotists, and even then we were aware of this fact. We listened and watched with skepticism.

Professor Sossamon began his program by explaining the mechanics of the abnormal psychology involved—muscular tiredness, total relaxation, willingness to be hypnotized. Then he called for volunteers to join him on stage. Some 25 or 30 students accepted his invitation, including my roommate, Ralph Sheppard, and my good friend Gordon Barbour. He sat them all on chairs in a semi-circle behind the lectern and, facing them, began speaking in a soothing but intense, persuasive manner. He asked them to rotate their forearms a minute or two, one way, then the other. They soon tired and relaxed. Walking back and forth slowly along the line he kept up his patter. "You're getting sleepy now, close your eyes, relax, soon you'll drop off to a deep, peaceful sleep."

Much to our astonishment it wasn't long until about 20 of our friends were sound asleep in their chairs. As the Professor had said, not all would be hynotized, and those who were not, including Gordon Barbour, left the stage and joined me in the audience.

At this point the Professor announced that he would bring the students from their trance into a "sonambulustic or sleep-walking state," and ask them to do various things. Approaching closely to a slumbering student Sossamon would talk to him in low tones and soon he would rub his eyes, seem to be awake, and the Professor would bring him to the front of the stage. Many of the "stunts" escape my memory, but I recall one fellow, Frank Penland, thinking and acting as if he were hoeing corn, chopping wood, picking cotton and milking a cow. Then he was told he was selling popcorn and peanuts and was sent down into the audience where he wandered about crying his wares in a somewhat plaintive voice. At one point three students were moving about among us thinking they were vendors of one sort or another.

Meanwhile Sossamon was explaining "post-hypnotic suggestion" and to illustrate brought Frank back to the stage, and emphasized to him that when he heard a sharp hand clap he was to jump up and crow like a rooster. Again in a low toned, intense voice and moving his hand in front of Frank's face, he brought him out of his hypnotic state and sent him to join us. A few minutes later, while Frank was laughing with the rest of us at the stage antics of his friends, the Professor clapped his hands and, indeed, Frank did jump up from his seat and crow like a rooster. As he slowly sat down with a sheepish grin on his face we were doubled over with laughter and amazement, and shouted requests for more stunts, which the Professor aimably accepted.

About this time he brought to the fore a good ol' boy from South Carolina, Jess Oates. After various exchanges which had us in stitches, Sossamon said "Jess, you are General Washington at Valley Forge. Your troops are cold, discouraged and beaten. You must inspire them. Get up there. Talk to them! He repeated his instruction. Slowly (in his normal manner, I should say) Jess ambled to the lectern and looked out on us. "Men," he began, then hesitated. The Professor murmured encouragement. "Men," he repeated emphatically, but in his sandlapper drawl, "Men, we've got to get back on our feet, and charge out there and beat the _____ out of those _____ damn Yankees!"

We shouted with laughter. Then, at our urging, he agreed to show us how the strange power of hypnosis would carry over with Jess until the next morning, a Sunday. Jess was a hearty eater and always had seconds which were permitted on Sundays. It was agreed that when he came back with his seconds and passed the chair of Tom Graham, Tom was to say to him "Jess, you're getting as fat as a Thanksgiving turkey." At this point Jess was to flap his arms and gobble like a turkey.

Those of us at Ross Hall hurried over to the dining room for breakfast that morning. All worked as planned, except that on signal, when Jess froze in his tracks, he dropped his tray, and started to flap and gobble, such a storm of hoots, yells and hollers swept the hall that Jess stopped in mid gobble and went on to his seat.

But let's get back to the auditorium. From the wing Professor had four fellows bring out a boulder which it took all four to lift. The subject from the drugstore window was now suspended between two chairs, heels on one, head on the other. Professor said he was in a cataleptic state, possessing unusual strength. The men placed the boulder on the man's stomach. Then he handed Joe an eight-pound sledge hammer and told him to strike the stone. Poor Joe. He was a ministerial student and a gentle, good-hearted fellow. He hit a few weak blows and when the man sagged a bit the Professor repeated his "rigid and stiff" instruction and slowly the man arched the stone back up. But Joe had had enough. The program had now exceeded two hours. Much as we had enjoyed ourselves, we were a little relieved when the Professor brought the sub-ject to normal consciousness and we saw that he now func-tioned normally. We gave him a big round of applause as he left the stage, having over-earned his $5.00.

Sossamon said he would bring the remaining students to a sleep-walking stage. He then told them they were enjoying a picnic in a beautiful meadow by a mountain stream. At that point he "lost" my room-mate, Ralph. Later, on the walk back to Ross Hall, he listened in disbelief as I told him what had gone on. When I asked him eagerly what he remembered he replied with keen disappointment, which I still remember, "Nothing, except I was about to enjoy a picnic with a beautiful girl and other girls all around (very important to Ralph) and everything was so clear and real, when suddenly I realized I was in the auditorium."

For several weeks after this program everyone read and talked about hypnotism. One student declared he had learned the skill and even "put on a show" at the next Delphinian Literary Society. Most of us Clios also attended. We quickly spotted him as a fake because for better or worse we had indeed seen the real McCoy!

—R.A. Stevenson, '36

❧

A Poet Speaks in Self Defense

I

Ancient man, short on fact, turned to fable for a crutch. Locked in his tight circle of ignorance, he sought to palliate fear and rationalize his dark-room existence by inventing explanation for his four-cornered world.

Eventually there grew up a mythology that soothed his frightened ego. He began to toy with the idea that there might even exist some Superior Intelligence, or Order, in his world. This helped him to build his railings more securely, fence along the edge.

Gradually he learned to arm himself against life's inevitable disappointments by adopting an "I can't lick you but my big brother can" attitude, suitably backed by obliging gods who fought his battles, held at bay the worst of his dragons. These super beings ranged the earth in perpetual duel with gargantuan evils who would destroy man.

Even so, survival was uncertain.

Today modern man has separated fact and fiction. He would be the first to tell you. His universe has become an exact science, answerable only to a slide rule, a robot Univac.

But despite apparent progress, man today, at least sociologically, is skating on *The Thin Ice*. He lives under constant nuclear threat of *The Falling Sky*. He gropes blindly, a hard-shelled beetle in a china cup, along the yawning raw edge of Space.

And there is still the haunting carry-over from his past: *Survival is uncertain.*

II

Literally for modern man, fiction has engulfed fact. Buck Rogers has finally overrun him. At the other end of the knowledge scale man is struggling desperately to find an anchorage, to stabilize sanity with some sort of commonsense mythology that can help him "rationalize" his continued exposure to the Cape-Canaveralized spectacular.

This bombardment has been more than enough to drive him, *en masse,* to the psychiatrist's couch. He doesn't have to catch "sight of Proteus rising from the sea" or "old Triton blowing his wreathed horn" to imagine that he is slowly going mad. He doesn't need to see Prometheus running with the stolen fire—he has only to look toward the beaches of Canaveral, where snorting dragons would scare the pants off anything but a hibernating, introvert ostrich. Clever comrades meantime promote a "cold war" that may lift him bodily at any moment "right out of this world."

More than ever his cave-cousin brother, Average Man today needs the poet, the weaver of tales. He needs the protective translucency of fable to help him soften his morning headlines, live through his next week's life. He needs music and laughter and song—not pep pills, popping corks and sedatives.

As man prepares to shed his fledgling wings like a pair of old outgrown longies, the more gracefully to take his place in the coming fourth dimension of interspace existence, a brand new complexity, that of the astounding Spaceman of the Twentieth Century—the Astronaut—begins to weave its spell about him.

While this is happening, even as much as the scientist, the poet needs to be there. For, surely, the Astronaut's strange transcendence into Space is an integral part of Everyman; and nowhere can its fantasy and its reality be more faithfully joined than through the ears and eyes and heart of the poet, in fable, ballad and song.

He is—Astronaut or Poet—both the chosen and the afflicted. He is in some small part what Everyman desires to be, sometimes unknowingly attempts to be, but doesn't quite bring off.

Bitter at times, the poet may long to shed his overly sensitive tentacles, or the Astronaut his destiny, and be just an Everyman. This cannot be. The leprosy, the acute loneliness, the nagging little echo from out the boundless deep of Time—these things are too deeply fixed.

But except for a dozen or so mental giants, Everyman cannot yet explain, much less begin to understand himself, in the bold, broad language of his destiny.

This is where feeling begins and poetry belongs—often long before there is written expression. One down-to-earth ballad can outweigh the most scholarly tomes of history, if it is a song that soothes the soul; for souls in peace put minds at ease. This, more than anything, man lacks.

Time doesn't need to pause. It's that hard-pressed animal, modern man, who needs occasional moments of quiet contemplation, alone with himself, to feed his ingrown, starving soul. Poetry can be one such food.

III

Sometimes in his smoke-filled dens this man creature is heard to boast that he is gradually acquiring an extra-sensory sixth sense, or awareness, like a bug's feelers, to make easier his earthly existence.

Our coming generation of Spacemen may also develop some yet-undreamed-of seventh formula in space-time-distance that will make interplanetary adventure as commonplace as today's jet travel.

At least there is note of this budding perception in our present-day six-year-olds. They would accept, casually as breakfast cereal, armies of little green men only six inches tall, if they stepped into America's living rooms through our television screens, tonight!

Flying saucers landing tomorrow in Chicago's Loop, and loaded with little Martians smoking famous brandname filter tips through their ears, would be accepted by many adults with, "Looky, the funny helicopters! What won't those ad boys think up next?"

Nor could Orson Welles ever pull another panic-antic, to save his sponsor's neck. His listeners would switch to Jack Paar, or kick the danged contraption's button and march nonchalantly off to bed.

IV

May be this *live dangerously, tomorrow we orbit* concept is the new culture cocoon of our coming space age. Who can say? At any rate, we do not have burden ourselves with the answers. It's the questions that shake us up!

As simply as Milton Berle would say, Why not? If Time stands still at the speed of light, as our modern medicine men assure us it does, then from our little cracker barrels we must feed a feeble sanity with new ideas, just to keep in step, mind you. One of mine goes something like this:

Time, multiplied by the speed of light factor, multiplied by a predetermined fraction of tic-toc-two, would back me up to the American Revolution, or wherever in Time I chose to go, simply by changing the fractional power input of the tic-toc-two over one. I could, simply stated, steer my little canoe backward up the Lakes Of Eternity, picnicking as I pleased.

I would be the proud owner of a new kind of compact, a Magamericar, nuclear driven perhaps; tail-finned, of course; and with meteorite repulsers, alternators, and moonbeam skids, chromed front and back.

As the man says, Why not? It makes as much sense, to me, as the Einsteinish kid who says that a yardstick is no more a yardstick in a space ship traveling at the speed of light, because it would change its form.

And I was taught in school that a leopard cannot change its spots!

Oh, well.

V

Who among us hasn't at some time felt himself the victim of Television, among the modern evils, or dreamed that he would like to chop down the antenna to end all antennas, like Jack who bean-whacked the old giant?

What mother hasn't shuddered at the thin ice of sex and social abandon on which we cavort so casually, cheek to cheek?

Who hasn't believed, even quarterly these days, that the dragons of taxation and political chicanery are swallowing us, hock and fetlock?

These are but warning cracks in *The Thin Ice;* the threats of our *Falling Sky.*

But, as I promised, no conclusions.

I present this little volume simply as a current model carry-it-with-you sandbox.

If horrible conclusions jump you, unbidden; if suddenly you see something sneaking up on you that looks like Aggy the Snaggy Old Witch only because it *is* Aggy, in person, riding her latest nuclear doom, then as a full-feathered fellow Ostrich I salute you. On my scout's honor I hasten to add:

Welcome to this space-age sandbox.

Quick! In here, Friend, with me!

$\mathcal{A}bout\ the\ \mathcal{A}uthor$

Leroy Sossamon was born November 15, 1912, on a Cabarrus county, N.C. farm. Growing up in the teeth of the Great Depression was a test of survival. No paved roads, indoor plumbing, electricity, or telephones. Almost no money. Nearest neighbor a mile away, two-room school 3 miles away.

By 17 he showed promise as a writer, speaker, picture in Time Magazine, and entered Appalachian, where he graduated cum laude in 1934 and started teaching English and French at state scale, $3 per day.

He loved teaching but made more during the summers than he made all year teaching and went into the furniture business, ending up with a chain of 9 stores. He gradually expanded into real estate, construction, and owned a newspaper which brought on a lengthy stand-off with some politicians. In 1982, risking everything, he purchased a textile company with 3 plants, 950 employees, a $42 million volume and $11 million in bankruptcy. Sossamon immediately downsized to two plants, 350 employees and in 3 years was solid and profitable.

Clinton and NAFTA later destroyed the Carolinas textile industry, and after yet another lengthy absense from his writing, Sossamon is back with his 4th book, MOUNTAINS

ARE FOREVER. His third, THESE MY MOUNTAINS, THIS MY LAND, with somewhat limited distribution, sold 10,000 copies. With this one, and more time to promote, he hopes to do better.

As mentioned in two short poems, THE TWO OF US and APOLOGIES (pages 222, 223), Sossaman has often been wedged between the PRACTICAL and the DREAMER. Now at an age when his mortality is coming more clearly into view, but the list of things yet to do grows longer for an ever shorter time, perhaps the DREAMER will once more emerge, and joining the PRACTICAL, well, Who knows! One more time? Maybe!

❧

Comments by Others About Sossamon's Work

BACKSIDE OF HEAVEN, 1959. For those who thrill to the majesty of mountain peaks and are deeply touched by the mingling of earth and sky in some lonely place of earth, this slender little volume of verse by Leroy Sossamon is enthusiastically recommended—It is a tender and delicate collection of exquisite verse—the kind that rings in the heart and is like a mellow bell to the ear.

There is none of this hocus-pocus, literary hanky-panky attempt at pseudo-intellectualism which characterizes so much verse. **It is simple, heartfelt and human with beautiful words capturing the mood of the western North Carolina Mountains as might an artist using soft pastel colors. . . .**

Mr. Sossamon may not get rich selling his book but he will have the satisfaction of knowing that he, at least, has added one more touch of sunshine to a world which too often is plunged into shadow. **J.B. Clark, the Charlotte (NC) Observer, 1959**

FALLING SKY, 1961. Leroy Sossamon is a remarkable person, and a poet of real ability. It is a wonderful thing to have this North Carolina poet of our Great Smoky Mountains, who creates such an inspiring poetry. **FALLING SKY** is appealing and rewarding. It is a delightful book. **Luther H. Hodges, U.S. Secretary of Commerce, 1961**

FALLING SKY, 1961. Sossamon shows a remarkable range of subject matter. Even as he glories in the thought of space travel he is aware of the possible consequences of conquering space.

> "If out in space at the speed of light
> Time stood still and nothing but night
> Stretched out from his Spaceship, world on end,
> Where would man turn? Who would be his friend?"

Sossamon proves himself to be an extraordinary facile and adroit writer. Too long has he remained in obscurity, for his is a most remarkable talent. His work is fresh and exciting, exhilarating and stimulating. He is a joy to read! **Greensboro (N.C.) Daily News, FALLING SKY, 1961**

THESE MY MOUNTAINS, THIS MY LAND, 1983. This is not only by all odds the best poetry of the week, but also may stake a claim to ranking with the best poetry of the year in the United States. That evaluation may be disputed by those who worship poetic emperors who—despite their denial—"wear no clothes."

It will dismay those who are so shocked at classic poetic imagery, at lines that scan and even—really!—verses that sometimes rhyme. Those who maintain that they, instead, are turned on by prose—really dull and plodding prose— chopped up in irregular lines, should avoid this book. It is only for those who esteem conventional poetry, salted with genuine folk expressions, a touch of religion, and occasional references to the Bible, and to Greek classics. The poems, as the title indicates, celebrate the wonder and beauty of the Southern

Appalachians. The subjects, however, span the range of personal philosophy, romantic love, folk narrative and senses of awe and wonder at encounters with nature. Out of such variety, one line displays the free range of Sossamon's expressive lines: "Perhaps down that other road in the yellow wood, Mr. Robert Frost, I'll meet up with you one day." And maybe he will. **20th CENTURY SOUTH, Augusta, GA, 1983**

Other Comments About the Mountain Poet
and His Work

25 July 83
Rt #10 Box 122A
Hagerstown, Md 21740

Dear Leroy,

After further reading, I am impelled to say: "you touched me."

James Kavanaugh, the former priest who stirred some circles when he laid aside his robes has written something that I feel could have been written just for you.

I treasure counting you among my friends.

Eric Nordling

There are men too gentle to live among wolves
Who prey upon them with IBM eyes

And sell their hearts & guts for martinis at noon.
There are men too gentle for a savage world
Who dream instead of snow & children & Halloween
And wonder if the leaves will change their color soon.

There are men too gentle to live among wolves
Who anoint them for burial with greedy claws
And murder them for a merchant's profit & gain.
There are men too gentle for a corporate world
Who dream instead of candied apples & ferris wheels
And pause to hear the distant whistle of a train.

There are men too gentle to live among wolves
Who devour them with eager appetite & search
For other men to prey upon & suck their childhood dry.
There are men too gentle for an accountant's world
Who dream instead of Easter eggs & fragrant grass
And search for beauty in the mystery of the sky.

There are men too gentle to live among wolves
Who toss them like a lost & wounded dove,
Such gentle men are lonely in a merchant's world,
Unless they have a gentle one to love.

Kavanaugh

August, 1961
2221 Westminster Place
Charlotte, N.C.

Sossamon:
    I think you are a GREAT Poet . . . The other day I was
down at Loftin's Press looking at Jonathon Williams' stuff

because I expect to bring him to my Queens College class on Dec. 14th. . . . While I was shuffling through these beautiful productions he has done of some fairly weak and worthless stuff, I came upon an unbound copy of FALLING SKY and sneaked out of there with the copy. This morning I have been rabidly cutting the pages and clapping out astonished approval of every page. How clear your ear! Go Sossamon! How vigorous and contrapuntal the click of those poems, and the song!

I want to talk. I want to know about you and why you have not published everywhere and what you are doing out there in Bryson City. And who is encouraging and damning your writing and who is selling your book. I am reviewing your book for the Charlotte Observer and would like a copy of *Backside of Heaven.*

You'll be, I suppose, curious about me as I am about you. I am a poet and love my craft. When I was fresh out of graduate school at Chapel Hill in 1956 my passion and technique was most fortunately exposed to the intensive concern and brilliant teaching of Ezra Pound. I taught on the English faculty at State College in 1957 and since then at Queens in Charlotte. I am sending you one of my poems because I respect your work and hope to hear from you soon.

Charleen Whisnant